BONUS: TEN EASY STEPS FOR ORGANIZING POLITICAL CHANGE

★ ★ ★ ★ ★ ★ ★ ★ ★ ★ ★ ★ ★ ★ ★

THE
STRATEGIC CITIZEN

A CITIZEN'S GUIDE TO PLAYING AND WINNING THE GAME OF POLITICS

★ ★ ★ ★ ★ ★ ★ ★ ★ ★ ★ ★ ★ ★ ★

GERRY PATNODE

Morgan James Publishing • New York

THE
STRATEGIC CITIZEN

ISBN: 978-1-60037-309-1 (Paperback)
978-1-60037-310-7 (Hardcover)

PUBLISHED BY:

Morgan James Publishing, LLC
1225 Franklin Ave Ste 325
Garden City, NY 11530-1693
Toll Free 800-485-4943
www.MorganJamesPublishing.com

GENERAL EDITOR:
Heather Campbell

COVER & INTERIOR DESIGN BY:
3 Dog Design
www.3dogdesign.net
chris@3dogdesign.net

TABLE OF CONTENTS

ACKNOWLEDGEMENTS

I want to acknowledge and thank the persons who without their support and encouragement, the research conducted to produce *"The Strategic Citizen..."* would not have been possible. First, I want to thank my research colleagues and mentors, Dr. Toni A. Gregory and Dr. Odis Simmons, both of Fielding Graduate University, who introduced me to a new way of viewing and interpreting the world through the use of Grounded Theory. I also wish to acknowledge the friendship, support and candor of my colleagues in the political arena especially, former Baltimore County Executives, Dennis F Rasmussen and Charles "Dutch" Ruppersburger, now a member of Congress, who provided candid assessments and allowed me the opportunity for unobstructed in-depth research and analysis. Additionally, I want to acknowledge the current and former public officials, community activists, community and business association executives, and community members, who gave me total access to the political process in their communities. Finally and perhaps most importantly, my wife, Nancy who encouraged, critiqued and supported this effort.

INTRODUCTION

In my life as both a player of the political game and a serious scholar of Leadership, it has been my observation, that in the beginning, the decision to enter public life is a noble gesture. Often, the newcomer to the political game is filled with idealism and good will. However, over time, the idealism and good will are replaced by an exercise in political survival. The process turns to a constant struggle to retain political power, not for the benefit of the public, but for maintaining ones position.

Political power is an aphrodisiac. Once an individual has experienced the narcotic effect of power in the public sector; they are, more times than not, consumed by its allure. They tend to crave more and higher levels of power. Just as the drunk; the politician does not easily relinquish the glass. However, citizens, acting as society's bartender, have the responsibility to cut off the patron who has consumed too much. Citizenship requires that we remain vigilant to the politician who enjoys the power to the exclusion of the people they serve.

My purpose for writing this book lies in two areas. The first, as an insider I have a unique perspective. Even though I was unable to rise in elected political position beyond township-community levels, I did attempt to move up the political food chain. Although defeated in my attempts, I was through my increased visibility, able to garner several appointed positions at the Federal, State and County levels. In these positions I found myself drinking from the same bottle of wine as my elected brethren. Upon retrospection, I found the process both rewarding and troubling. It is in that light that the second reason for this book emerged. Citizens must understand that politics is a game. For those of us who play the game, we recognize that it is a contact sport with a set of unique and sometimes hidden rules of engagement.

The problem for the average citizen is that first, they are disengaged from the political process. In addition, even when they attempt to join the political game, they do not understand the nature of the game and they most certainly don't understand the rules. This uncharted realm is confusing and is partly the reason citizens don't bother to engage. As I will demonstrate later, this is a state of affairs which the seasoned politico hopes continues. In fact, many politicos will find ways to foster the general citizen's disengagement from the political process.

When a citizen seeks to influence a political decision, they in most cases have no concept of the process that will cause any favorable action. Politicians and bureaucrats will utilize their own particular brand of a cost benefit analysis before any action is taken. The calculated outcome will determine whether a politician finds merit to address a person's concerns. They weigh first whether seeking a solution is politically desirable. What should be understood is that political decision making is different from the approaches taken by those not involved in the political process. Knowing and appreciating that difference is crucial in leveling the playing field and understanding the rules in the game of politics.

The positions I take within these pages are based on my personal experience and observations coupled with extensive primary research. The result is an insight into the political mind's calculus. These pages offer a look at the dynamics of political behaviors. The citizen self-defense options and solutions offered are all field tested.

The starting point for the initial research was an interest in understanding the types and dynamics of behaviors exhibited by political leaders and the impact of those behaviors on the political process and decision making at the community level. Even as an insider, I was sometime mystified by how hard it was to get anything accomplished. I am deeply interested in discovering why substantial progress in attacking persistent social problems rarely occurs and why change within the political and social scene is for the most part resisted. I simply decided to understand, why?

The truth of the matter is that we are constantly plagued with the same repeating problems; such as, the failure to fix social security, poverty, and education deficiencies.

In order to get at the core of political reasoning, I chose to use my personal knowledge combined with a sociological research methodology known as grounded theory. This methodology allows for incredible insight into behaviors and social process even by those intimately engaged in the process under study. The method, developed by Bernie Glaser Ph.D., of the University of California, allowed for the emergence of a theory from the collected data. The models of behavior and processes presented here help to describe and explain the dynamics of political leadership and the decision process of politicians.

At the core of the presented model, is a central behavioral variable, which I have named "Shoring-up". The understanding of the dynamics of this behavioral variable and of the resultant process model derived from it, allows for a greater understanding of political decision-making and the ramifications for individuals, groups, government officials, communities and public institutions. Shoring-up is a behavior exhibited by political leaders as part of their problem-solving process. The behavior of Shoring-up has the goal of diffusing opposition and insuring the continued support of critical constituencies for the sole purpose of retaining political power and control.

To help the reader achieve some basic understanding of the research methodology used as a basis for explaining the behaviors and processes in this book, Grounded Theory is an inductive research tool rather than a deductive approach. The approach gives the researcher a systematic method for examining complex social issues. It provides a set of strategies for collecting, and analyzing data. The Grounded Theory process requires the researcher to remain open to the emergence of relevant theory that is derived from the data as opposed to testing some logically elaborated hypothesis as found in the deductive approach.

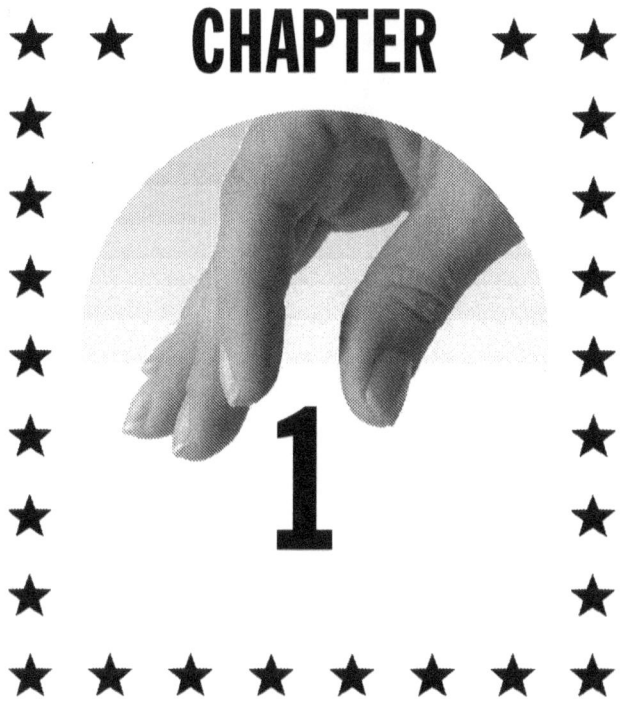

CHAPTER 1

Unlocking the Puzzle of
Politics and Political Power

Chapter 1

Unlocking the Puzzle of Politics and Political Power

We cannot assume today that men must in the last resort be governed by their own consent. Among the means of power that now prevail is the power to manage and manipulate the consent of men. That we do not know the limits of such power—and that we hope it does have limits—does not remove the fact that much power today is successfully employed without the sanction of the reason, of the conscience of the obedient.

– C. Wright Mills

The Issue

I am thankful that you have made a decision to explore the ideas and concepts on the following pages. The understanding of the political process and your potential role in that process is important for the political health of our nation. Too few citizens take that interest, but I have hope that the numbers will continue to grow.

I believe the future of America and perhaps the world depends upon a re-engagement of Americans in the political process. I suspect that you are someone who cares greatly about your country and community. As such, I am going to give you the brutal facts and the reality of how political life really works and how it directly effects you and everyone you hold dear. Even though you may care, you struggle to make sense of the puzzle of political process. You probably are someone who also struggles to understand the rationale of decisions made by those who hold public leadership positions.

Perhaps you are even someone who toys with the idea of becoming a more involved citizen as an activist or community organizer but don't see how you can make a difference. Maybe you even toyed with the thought of running for public office but have no idea how or where to start. If any of these fit, I wrote this for you, but even if you are just someone who has asked the question; "why do the same issues and problems seem to be present year after year without resolution?" This effort may just help answer that question.

Who among us has not thought that the solutions to many of our social problems seem obviously clear, but yet, as a society we find it impossible to solve. Have you ever asked yourself; why can't, or more accurately, why won't our politicians do something? I believe that my analysis will help you fully understand the dynamics of the answer. I sometimes ask, given track records, "How do these people get elected?" The real question may be, given our track record of non-involvement, "don't we have the political leaders we deserve?"

Truth is, under the current "game" most of us believe that we don't have the time, energy, or skills to deal with the political process. It is a tacit recognition that most citizens haven't a clue as to not only "what to do" but "how to do it". The problem is that most of us feel that we don't have any control over what happens or over what "they" do. I am here to tell you that that attitude and assumption is dead wrong! Furthermore, I want you to know flat-out, that such a belief puts America at risk.

You have the ultimate control. What you don't have is an understanding of the informal process we refer to as politics. Depending when you went to high school, you, if lucky, were at least taught basic civics of how the formal governing process supposedly works. I am totally confident that unless you too are a "routine player" in the game politics that you don't know the informal process. I am also willing to bet that you are unaware that an informal process even exists.

How things work

It is true that we can't easily change the system, but what we can change is how we react to, and interpret what happens within the system. We have an ability to have some impact on the informal system processes. The really big things in political life tend to be accomplished within the informal system.

I will spend considerable time describing the political behaviors around making decisions. I offer a detailed description of a mostly unseen political process.

Secondly, I offer a prescription for how to bring about political change. While most of what I offer lends itself to or is about local political process, the truths uncovered here are true from the local to the international political arena. The rules and processes used by politicians are universal at all levels.

Politicians and the bureaucrats that run the government are responsive to only one thing. That is political pressure that threatens to undermine their power base. Threats to power will always get their attention. Politicians are not secure in their role. If citizens want to get favorable reactions from politicians, they must learn to use the fact that politicians are insecure. While most love the process of getting elected, the skills needed for staying in power are difficult work. The activist seeking change or political favors can use that fact to make positive things happen. However; you need to know the secrets of how politicians think and know the hidden rules of the game in order to play at the "professional" level.

I have developed a simple model offered for your understanding. It better identifies and explains a typical politician's behaviors when they are presented social and political problems. Having the knowledge of these behaviors allows potential activists to understand that when you want something from a politician, you must make it important to the politician on a very personal level. Quite frankly, your issues if not important to them on a personal level are simply unimportant.

Taking Control

If you're ready to gain an understanding of the rules for the game of politics and ready to become an effective catalyst for political change, I am ready to lead the way. It is now time to change not only your misperceptions but to give you the skill to play and win the game of politics.

To be fair, you should recognize that your guide and mentor into this journey is what must be considered a recovering politician. Truth be told, I'm not sure that I won't relapse. The allure to the game is hard to get out of ones system once they have tasted the fruits of the game. I have run for office. I love to campaign. It's a narcotic for those who love the "grin, greet and grab" of wading into a crowd. I have been elected to office and have been defeated in attempts at higher office. In retrospect, I am now convinced that my political loss came as a result of the collective wisdom of the citizens of Baltimore County. I have also breathed the rarified air of politically appointed positions at the Federal, State and local level.

In my conversations with my fellow non-politically engaged citizens, I am struck by the general feeling of their believed powerlessness. They believe that under the current state of affairs, we are at the mercy of our political leaders. The sad truth is that until citizens take an active role in our democracy, we are at the mercy of our own inaction.

Rediscovering Citizenship

The future for winning the political game, particularly on the local government levels lies in transforming passive consumers of public services into responsible citizens. The demands of time and the complexity of problems facing communities,cause many to sullenly withdraw from the political process. This is a withdrawal from their civic responsibilities. Instead, many make unrealistic demands on local government officials without regard to the complexities. This in turn forces these same government officials, in order to save their perches of power, to engage in the negative behaviors that we will explore in the following pages.

I will shortly introduce you to the concept of political "Shoring-up". Most certainly you have been exposed to the practice of Shoring-up. Whether you recognized it at the time as such, it has been performed to and on you. It is for this reason that we will fully explore this universal political behavior and will fully explore the triggers and mechanisms of the Shoring–up process. These outcomes are designed to keep the average citizen on the sidelines of the playing field. My hope is that once this political behavior is recognized, that it will easily be defused. This will be a necessary action if any real progress is to be made in actually solving political and social problems.

Interestingly, for citizens to be "shored up" against, they must allow themselves to become powerless and non-factors in the decision process of politicians. In effect, we allow for our own disenfranchisement. We surrender our civic roles through political disengagement. Citizenship is not limited merely to voting in periodic elections.

Frank Benest, (November, 1996.) *International City/ County Management Association Journal* suggests; "Even when individuals do not have a personal stake, active citizenship requires them to:

★ Inform themselves on key issues confronting their communities.

★ Participate in civic improvement groups.

★ Struggle to find common ground with others, as well as advocate their private interests.

★ Become responsible for their local governments and their communities"

Ultimately, cities and counties cannot govern and cannot solve complex problems if people are merely passive consumers. The community leader and political activist has a vital role if America is to continue as we know it. The activist citizen is not only needed as the political antagonist, but they have a role in engaging more people into becoming responsible citizens.

Politicians would like nothing better than to have citizens as non-participants. That would mean a lack of need for accountability.

More importantly, for those that accept the challenge of leadership, it is vital to understand how to take control of the political process. This means being able to recognize, understand and intervene effectively in the political process. In short-you need to know how to play the game.

What has changed?

I am certain that the founding fathers would not recognize the democratic republic they formed. First, they would be horrified at the strength of the central government and the unconstitutional role of the courts in mandating and creating law versus interpreting law.

They would also not understand the concept of politics as a career. The envisioned citizen legislator as a temporary period of community service left the scene during the Lincoln administration and the concept of state's and community rights began their journey away from what the founding fathers had created.

It was at this time politicians discovered the emerging apathy of the American voter. This apathy allowed a few activist citizens and the political leaders that pandered to their needs to set in place the informal political system as we see it today. Just in case you haven't gotten the truth about how our political systems work, here it is pure and simple. Less than ten percent of the adult population controls 100% of the political process and rewards those who do their bidding. Why is this true? We as a political collective have become…well fat, dumb and lazy because we are comfortable. We get just enough to keep us from rioting in the streets. As we sit in our stupor of un-involvement, the eroding of our civil liberties happens just like the bull frog in a pot of consistently warming water. He sits there until his butt is cooked. Without the rediscovery of our civic roles, Americans can start looking for the fork. We are almost done.

I am of the opinion that the vast majority of citizens would not be happy at that prospect. Even if we were to suddenly understand that we are being ruled by an existing power elite, we seem to be too paralyzed to act.

The issue is that on some level we are apathetic. We fall to the 'not my direct problem' mode. Additionally, we are paralyzed into inaction because we don't how to proceed. We have been lulled or marginalized into a trap that allows the power brokers to play the game with us on the sidelines.

Examples of hope

The example of the new minutemen of the American southwest have proven that we can protect our borders and inhibit, intimidate and just plain stop the "illegals" from crossing over into Texas and Arizona in spite of the best political efforts to ignore the ninety percent of the population who desire to secure the borders.

It's that pesky ten percent that keeps the border open. These are the politically involved folks. These are people, who most likely own businesses needing cheap labor. This cheap labor keeps cost down and profits up enough to fund their favorite politician who works hard to keep their favor and their political contributions.

It is time to reclaim America for the majority of Americans. The ability to regain control lies in our collective ability to understand what is going on, and who is at the controls. This is accomplished first by making the commitment to take control. Second, is to know what and how to effect political change.

CHAPTER

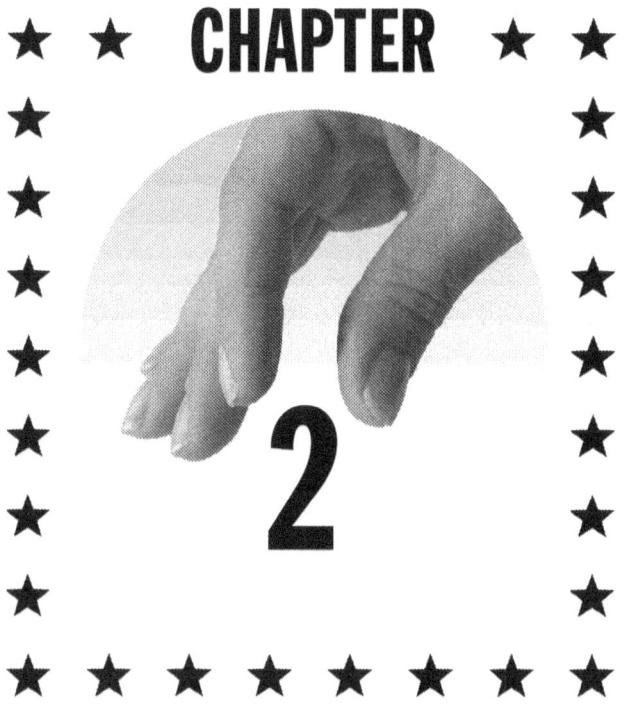

2

Wishing for Change
is not Enough

Chapter 2

Wishing for Change is not Enough

We are not likely to change the political system in one life time. It took two-hundred years to distort. Social systems change slowly and not all at once but in incremental steps.

In any attempt to orchestrate change, we need to think in terms of managing the process within the current system. It is also useful for future strategy development to understand how change happens. This too is a designed and orchestrated process. The process of "change management" from my perspective can be interpreted in two ways.

The first is an individuals' or organizations' ability to cope with and process change. This is change thrust upon them by some external set of factors. In short, learning to accept and live with change even if it has a negative effect on your life. This is the process of adaptation.

The Second, and the one to be examined here, is the process of making change happen in some planned and systematic fashion. The aim is to change how the system processes affect you. You then intervene in the process so that something different occurs within the existing system thereby effectively creating a new sub-system that supports your political or social goals.

For the average citizen forced to deal with the instability of political environments, it is more common for us to have developed the skills at coping with what has been dealt rather than attempting to create change. It is increasingly more important for the public to change that dynamic for the sake of preserving the original vision for our republic. We typically distinguish between knee-jerk reaction responses associated with coping, versus the proactive response indicative of managing change.

The management of proactive change requires a brief understanding of and knowing that a scholarly and applied body of knowledge for implementing change does exist. The knowledge consists of models, methods, techniques and other tools that can be called upon to develop and implement a change process and strategy. The context for this knowledge is drawn from the theories and approaches found in psychology, sociology, business, engineering, human and organizational behavior.

For the professional change agents, this process is linked and integrated into what has been part of our discussion of interventions within existing systems. The basics in understanding methods and consequences of various interventions is essential for anyone seeking to create system change.

Communities are highly specialized systems just as any corporate organization and no two are exactly alike although they all have some commonalities.

When we approach the concept of community and political change, the process has been characterized as having three basic components or stages.

These stages are "unfreezing", "changing" and "refreezing". This draws heavily upon the work of Kurt Lewin in his systems concept of homeostasis or dynamic stability. In plain English- destabilize, implement change- stabilize the new process and system.

The major benefit of this work in exploring the process of political interventions and change is that it gives us a framework for developing staged approaches to instituting change. It allows the political and community activist a format to use for looking, learning and planning, before leaping. Probably the only downside to Lewin's approach is that it demands a certain system or organizational stability that is often non existent in the chaos of political environments; but even at that, knowing how the political and community systems operate is useful in our understanding of process within the organization or system.

The domain of Organizational Systems
The Arena of Political Decisions

The process of political decision making does not happen in a vacuum. The political process could be considered the "grease" within human organizational systems that lubricates the mechanisms to keep things operating. For our purposes, know that systems are designed for those for whom it benefits. When we think we observe dysfunctional systems, it merely illustrates that we are not the designed beneficiaries of the system's design. Political systems are designed for the benefit of the politicians and those who support them. All others are left to mount campaigns and issues to garner enough support to re-design the system for their benefit. In essence, we don't really change the political system, just our position within the system. The objective becomes dislodging place holders. As an example, think of the "Republican Revolution" in 1994; in which out of power Republicans mounted a national campaign to win the majority in the Congress of the United States. While pledging to "change the system and rid it of corruption"; all that really happened was that the players changed positions and everything stayed the same. We just traded one set of power holders for another. In 2006, the Democratic Party revised the system to their benefit and took control of the Congress.

If citizens choose to engage in political actions, they need to understand the structures of the systems in which the action takes place. Whether it is the community structure, political party structure or a community association; knowing how the system works will allow the strategic design for effective interventions.

A community system can in its most basic form be considered an input-out put model. This type community system's operating processes extract resources from the external environment and use them to produce a level of community wellness. This wellness is the output of the community processes. A desire to change any part of the input, processing or outcome requires an ability to break these three areas into the system component parts. Without this knowledge, it is impossible to develop interventions for change.

The extracted resources are then used by the community, public and economic institutions to produce the outputs that are required by the community. The outputs are both tangible and intangible and deliver the quality of life which members of the community desire.

When community systems fail to provide value for its members, an imbalance occurs within the system. We see a shift from a continued state of social equilibrium, to a condition of disequilibrium. As we will see later, this contributes to a state of "Political Tension" that will require political attention and action. In order for the citizen activist to ferment change, they will require the skills necessary to purposely create this situation. That requires knowing all the parts and interactions of the community and political system.

It is precisely this process that can be used later to create "purposeful disequilibrium". It is this disequilibrium that leads political leaders to seek actions and engage in behaviors that address any directed political pressure. For the activist seeking to get the attention of a political leader, purposeful disequilibrium is the preferred state which the activist wants to establish to force favorable political action.

It is this disequilibrium that leads political leaders to seek actions and engage in behaviors that I now have identified as "Shoring-Up" behaviors.

Getting Local...Your community system

Former Speaker of the House, Tip O'Neil, once remarked that all politics are local. It is for this reason I begin the examination of political systems at the community level.

The community system is in effect the playing field for initial political activity. It is a logical beginning for understanding how the political system functions and reacts to various interventions into a community's system processes. If we are to avoid the unintended consequences of our actions, it is important to appreciate that any attempt to correctly design corrective interventions is dependent upon how well we have understood how a particular community system operates.

In its generic form a system is a collection of parts interrelated to perform some function or achieve some goal. Systems by definition have input functions, a processing function and outcomes with ongoing feedback.

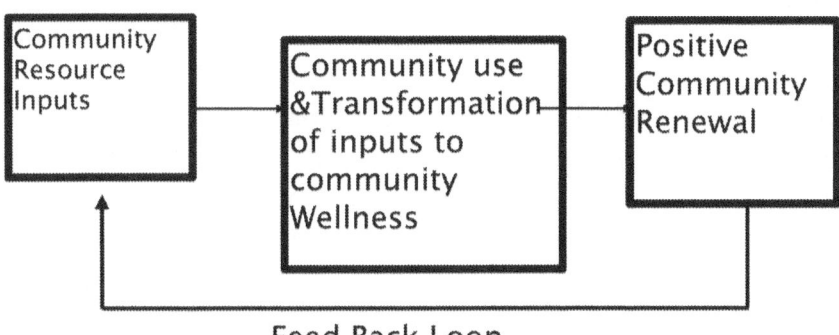

Feed Back Loop

If any part of the system is changed in anyway or removed, whether it is by design or to a default mode through inaction, the system is changed and relationship between the associated parts is also changed. What now exists becomes a new system with new rules and processes (Thompson, 1969).

The basic community design will have groups of components that satisfy the input, process, output function and a feedback / communications loop that will cause inputs to adjust to the demands of the community at large in satisfying quality of life issues. Should any of these components become a negative impact on the community creating political dis-equilibrium; a political action on the part of the effected political leaders will occur.

The preceding diagram is representative of a typical community system. Seeing the community as a system is beneficial in that it forces community planners and those engaging in problem solving to bring a new perspective in the interpretation of patterns and events within the community as opposed to a focus on single issues or events.

As I previously stated, social systems are designed for the benefit of someone or some group. The origins of the current design are essential to understanding if activists are to cope with the system dynamics, while introducing change. Instead of focusing on one symptom or a limited aspect of a problem, a systems approach forces a look at the whole system as links and causal effect processes. It is possible that component parts of the system work just fine on an individual basis; but when these components are integrated into the whole system and become interdependent, we sometimes see an unintended change. The use of a systems approach forces a look at all the parts and the feedback loop process that identifies system inefficiencies, or other undesirable functions.

Why all this systems thinking stuff?

The use of systems thinking in defining and analyzing human systems is a relatively new approach. The importance to this approach is a belief that the task of gaining political advantage for any group of citizens is impossible without knowing the workings of the community system process. The observation of natural systems and man's attempt at understanding the nature of the universe can be traced back to the first conscious recognition of the existence of the stars, moon and sun and the constant and predictable relationships between them. The desire of humans to explain or make sense of the surrounding environment has also inevitably led to man's desire to intervene and change his surroundings. Our preoccupation with the need to control or change things is demonstrated not only within our human systems but also in our efforts to challenge natural systems. We attempt to change everything from the course of rivers to the re-engineering of our basic genetic structure.

Given such pre-occupations, it would seem to be a natural extension for the social/political activist to notice that political change requires an analysis of what the system is and how it operates. This obviously ends in efforts to change the social system to a preferred change.

The use of a systems approach to understanding both simple and the most complex relationships can therefore refer to the smallest "whole" or to the entire universe. In fact, the systems approach can help us understand atoms, cells, man, families, committees, corporations and governments. The use of a systems approach to understanding both natural and human systems and more importantly as a diagnostic tool for interventions has proven to be a tempting tool in the management and development of organizations.

The potential usefulness of a systems should be appreciated as a powerful diagnostic tool. I will demonstrate throughout the following examples why looking at the whole is more important that dealing with component parts.

In the realm of business, education and government, the most promising use of the systems approach is in the area of building efficient human organizations. Applying a systems approach to analyses of organizations gives the citizen-activist cohesion to disparate facts and the relationship between systems enhancing problem definition and solving abilities.

Community Systems are "Open" Systems

A community is an example of an open system. Open systems are defined as having the three major perspectives of being open, rational and natural (Katz and Kahn, 1966). The characteristics of an open system are; self-maintenance based on a process of resources from the environment, and interaction with the external environment. Katz and Kahn summarize that an open system approach begins with the identification and mapping the repeating cycles of inputs, transformation, output and renewed inputs which comprise the organizational patterns.

Organizational systems, as a class of open systems, have properties of their own but share in characteristics common to all open systems. These as expressed as the importation of energy from the outside environment (inputs), transformation of inputs (process), and an end product of value (output) which is exported to the environment in exchange for more inputs. This approximates the basic model offered by Thompson. It is these elements that a political intervention seeks to influence or change.

Natural systems include social and political communities. These type organizations will develop a system on their own even if no formal governance structure is in place. Participants of the community share a common interest in the survival of the system and will engage in collective activities and informal structures that will insure that the community achieves acceptable levels of wellness.

GERRY PATNODE

CHAPTER

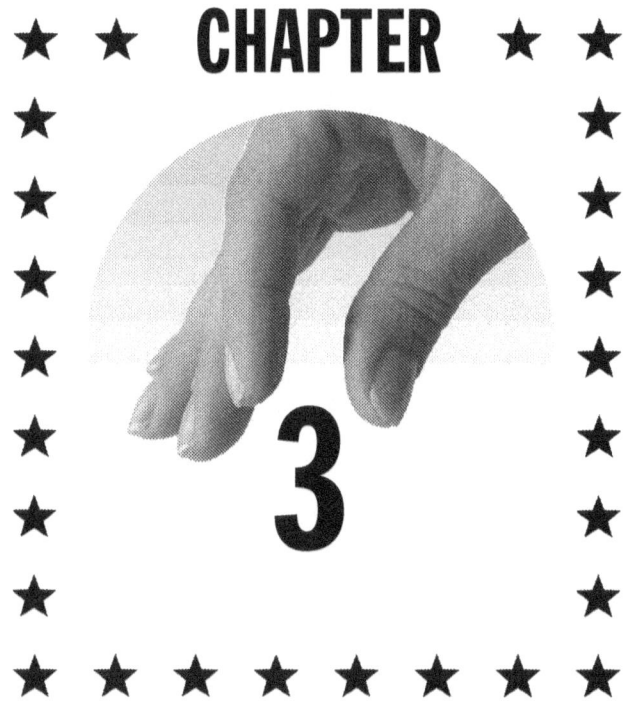

3

Change Requires Action

Chapter 3

Change Requires Action

The first step in effecting a change to the political status quo is a willingness to attack the entire system and not just the symptomatic parts that have attracted our attention. In addition, recognize that single issue attempts to make change rarely work. This means finding complimentary issues or at least non competing issues that can be joined into a more powerful political change force. Hopefully you will recognize the value of this approach as we proceed.

First, for the benefit of social and political activists; a social system failure is any change in the status quo that is viewed as detrimental to the perceived short or long term "wellness" of the community. In short, something has changed that negatively effected the quality of life for some segment of the community population.

To illustrate the importance of viewing change as a total systems issue, I have chosen to utilize the concept of systems archetypes as introduced by Peter Senge in "The Fifth Discipline". Systems Archetypes are basic and understandable cycles that systems go through. They are instructive in understanding how problems arise through unintended outcomes when the entire system is not attacked in addressing social problems. The use of archetypes can be found in various works on social systems.

Applying the use of archetypes can be useful in gaining insight into the nature of community systems and the underlying problems that lead to a system imbalance or dysfunction. Such imbalances traditionally divert the systems functions from the purpose of the originally designed system. By using typical system interventions currently in use by most politicians, or attempted by activist community members, we see the folly of addressing only the symptomatic elements of social problem in the social system.

The archetypes that are thought to offer the most insight into how systems change with various interventions are examined below. It will also be helpful to utilize an example of political process with the use of a partially contrived case study example. For the purpose of illustration, I have developed a case study that is a composite of communities located in Maryland. The composite communities have been given the fictitious names of Hill Top and Lakeside. The use of a case study allows for some flexibility and efficiency in describing mostly factual information combined with some logical elaboration on my part to illustrate a point. It is also necessary to provide anonymity to the participants. Although some are public figures, many are not. An explanation of the community operating system of both Hill Top and Lakeside provides insight into the elements that contribute towards community wellness.

The specific standard archetypes utilized are known as; "Shifting the Burden", "Eroding Goals", "Success to the successful", "Tragedy of the Common", "Fixes that Fail" and the "Attractiveness Principle". These system archetypes will help identify common system functions, interactions and the result of specific interventions. As you read the description of these actions, I am sure you can think of many situations within your own communities that have taken the same approach to problem solving with the same unfortunate results.

Shifting the Burden archetype is defined as a short term attempt to attack the symptoms of the real problem. It is my observation that this method of system correction is one of political expediency and one that is easily seen and demonstrated in any community. It allows the political pressure to lessen and is a cost effective approach. It is a process to divert enough resources to dampen the political fire and move the attention or focus towards other issues.

Eroding Goals archetype is similar to Shifting the Burden. It too is an approach to sanitize or create the illusion of a fix. In the communities under examination, community leaders and politicians both recognized that schools must appear to be meeting the performance goals. When not met the easier approach is to change the standard to a lower and easier to achieve level.

Success to the Successful archetype is a standard system phenomenon that directs resources to where it is least needed but most likely to be visibly successful. As an example, the herd mentality of investors is to invest where things are already investment winners, not recognizing that by that time the incremental value has peaked. The better investment is where investments are needed and currently at the low point with better upside value.

Tragedy of the Commons archetype is a consequence of an attempt at creating economies of scale without thought as to the effect that sharing resources may have on the system parts or competing systems. This process can cause system performance to erode and effects the sharing components will also experience declining performance. Some would legitimately say that our military system has experienced this in the war in Iraq.

Fixes that Fail is a very similar to the Shifting the Burden with a notable difference. This situation always has unintended consequences based on a lack of knowledge and understanding of the sub-system's interaction with the larger system environment.

Attractiveness Principle archetype takes its name from the process of selection. In terms of systems intervention, it is the process of deciding what symptom to attack first based on the resources available to mount an action. It is a process that has constraints or limits which force selection of elements of the problem deferring a full systems approach.

A Community Case Study with the Concepts Applied. In this case study example, two concepts are introduced as the action component of our archetypes. The first is the single issue action approach to addressing complex social issues. As will be demonstrated, this approach is generally too narrowly focused to offer permanent fixes. Yet it is usually politically expedient and lessens the political pressure in the short term. The action which addresses the situation is preventative in that it seeks only to establish or maintain political equilibrium.

The second is the previously mentioned political leadership behavioral concept - "Shoring-up." Shoring-up as will be seen in detail later, is a group of prescribed behaviors which are initiated when certain conditions are present. These behavioral actions are designed to defer any attempt at permanent solutions because the obtainment of a solution holds enormous political jeopardy. We can also clearly see how these approaches to decision-making are a reflection of the system archetypes.

Case History

The examples below are real but have been compressed into two communities from multiple communities studied in Maryland.

The composite communities were experiencing a noticeable decline in what is described as their community wellness factors. These include the issues of economic stability and general quality of life. Within our case communities, these same dimensions were under assault due to an aging infrastructure, demographic changes, economic decline and social changes that when combined showed a change in the basic quality of life previously enjoyed by these communities. The fictitious communities of Hill Top and Lake Village are typical of edge communities throughout America which have matured and are in close proximity of major cities. As such political leaders, who included county council members, the county executive and state legislative delegates were under considerable public pressure from several organized interest groups to stop and reverse the deterioration of these communities and improve the quality of life.

Symptoms experienced in these communities consisted of rising property crime, closing of retail businesses, declining property values and a drop in student performance in the community elementary and middle schools. These same conditions and situations have been demonstrated throughout the United States (Rusk. 1999). This set of circumstances and conditions changed the political environment to a state of disequilibrium.

In an effort to regain a state of equilibrium and lessened political tension, the political leadership needed to restore the leader follower dynamic of confidence and support. Generally this means needing to have the majority of support from the community's active persons. As I will continuously remind you, this is usually about ten-percent of the total adult population. As stated earlier, that means that five percent plus one person of the entire population is controlling public policy. The situation was made more difficult from a political position because the groups competing for favor and political resources tended to be grouped along racial lines which is always a highly charged emotional issue. The tension was created when one minority faction was blamed for the rise in crime, lowering of property values and the decline in school performance. This set of circumstances made any political action fraught with danger for the political leader and the community groups.

Community data collected generally supported community leader's assessment that overall community wellness was showing signs of stress. The downward trend was documented over a three year period. The issues creating the tension from elements within the community were that home sales in terms of units sold and the average sales price was rapidly declining while surrounding areas were enjoying a robust real estate market with rising prices.

The difficulty of selling a home in either Hill Top or Lake Village added to home owners bailing out and selling to investors who converted from owner occupied to renter units. This ownership change became a concern since it changed the basic character of the communities. With the increase in rental occupancy, the communities saw increases in violent and property crime in each community. Finally, the aggregate tax base for each community was declining with the property values. Nothing gets political attention more than the threat of a lessening of tax revenue.

The need to engage in some visible activity to relieve the mounting tension was precipitated by the pressures being exerted on politicians by the community associations and other community power groups that demanded action on the issues.

Remember my original premise is that political officials will seek to lessen the political pressure but not necessarily by solving the problem. The action taken by political leaders was to increase police presence by reducing police presence in adjoining communities. As a result, police patrols were increased resulting in higher arrests but no measurable decrease in the crime rate for the calendar year. To the contrary, property crime increased in Lakeside while personal crime remained the same. The results in Hill Top showed that the levels remained the same. Additionally, property values and the aggregate tax base continued to decline because of the perception of a worsening crime problem as witnessed by the increased police activity.

Community leaders who routinely supported the current political leadership complained that an undesirable element was moving into the community bringing crime and property deterioration with them. These community leaders forced the introduction of additional police action. Not surprisingly, emerging opposition groups countered that increased police activity was targeting a minority community group for no other reason than race. Outside groups, such as, the NAACP and the ACLU joined in the process creating a more powerful alliance with minority groups. Political leader's reacted to lessen tension. This was accomplished by political slight of hand creating the illusion of action. Through the creation of a community study commission, community leaders from all factions were asked to explore new approaches for solving the problem.

While to the politically naïve, this may seem a logical approach; it was designed to lessen the immediate pressure and refocus on a process with no ability to enact change but only to recommend an approach. This move effectively moved the politicians from the immediate line of fire and kept their support groups in a lessened state of tension for an extended time period. It is important to note that at no time was the issue of cause and effect relationships examined by this commission but only short term tactical decisions to address the symptoms. This was a political process made in heaven as far as the elected officials were concerned.

In reality, the most significant output from this community study commission was to recommend political action to stop or impede the emerging trends, not to address the real causes. You can see that we are back to the political game of inclusion and exclusion. The willingness of the political powers to allow a change in the community system evolved into actions designed to make community membership more difficult for new entrants into the community. New ordinances made selling residential property to investors nearly impossible or financially onerous. This cut down the availability of rental housing which discouraged those groups that could not afford to enter the community via home ownership. This created other problems within these community systems. The lack of buyers for homes for sale forced county leadership to Shore-Up relationships with the older residents who had political voting clout. As a result, new home buying assistance was funded by the county to help young family groups buy the available housing. Under normal community life cycling, this would, in the normal community evolutionary process, be a positive precursor for community renewal.

In contrast, the influx of families proved to be from poorer socio economic locations with school age children who happened to be academic under achievers. This situation brought a decline in performance on standardized test scores by students in the community's schools. This in turn seems to have kept the more upwardly mobile younger family buyers away from these communities. The plain truth is that bad schools do not attract good families.

The continued attraction of new residents from the poor urban areas of the state continued. They had fled city schools in favor of the better but declining county schools. This caused the communities to further deteriorate. The urban poor and economically disadvantage sought a relative improvement in the now declining county schools over the urban city school system.

Now let's examine what political leaders were forced to address and the results of their actions. First, by examination of those community attributes that define community wellness, we have declining communities. Political leaders were careful to frame the problems not as the poor ethnic minorities that moved into the area but the "evil" real estate investor. The potential for "inviting" the NAACP and the ACLU to enter the problem was averted by this important refocus. The fragmented and the perceived rich group of real estate investors from outside the community was an easy target to vilify. The approach was really a touch of political genus. If a way could be found to limit or stop the influx of poor minority families into the area; the perceived cause of new crime would be eliminated without a direct attack on a demographic group that has the ability to attract strong political advocacy groups. Through the use of the legislative process, new laws were created that made transforming single family homes into rental property an onerous exercise that soon stripped the profits from the investment.

Of course this action dried up real estate sales causing another out roar from the aging white middle class home owners who still wanted to leave the area. The situation forced an alliance with this group and groups representing the poor minorities that were now excluded from living in the community. This coalition became a formidable political action group. They were able to force politicians to address the issue by creating a pool of funds supplied by area banks seeking to comply with new Community Development Act regulations that could assist previously unqualified families in buying the available homes in the community.

While it was politically expedient to address the pressures from activists, the actions taken still did not address the core issue that started this whole process, which were increased crime and more police actions. If you are starting to feel that this is sounding like that old children's folk song of "There Was a Little Old Woman Who Swallowed a Fly", and eventually ended by swallowing a goat; it is not accidental. With all the dimensions of this community's problems emerging, political leaders are forced to find short term solutions to address the symptoms enough to get the political pressure defused or diverted to something else. In this case the approach made both political and solution sense. An attempt was made to stabilize the community and address those pressures that had the highest potential for posing a threat to the local politicians involved. Those homeowners in the community found a way to limit renters and therefore undesirables. Those wishing to sell (the no longer committed) found a way to sell. The political/social groups, like the NAACP and the ACLU, were appeased enough to give ground since people of color were now able to buy property in the community with government assistance.

Even with the skillful Shoring-up by the community's political leadership, we saw the community confronted with yet another problem created from the past decisions. The new political equilibrium sowed the seeds of further community deterioration. The influx of lower socio-economic groups into the community via the new ownership programs had a negative impact on the local schools. With limited preparation and poor academic skills, these children from city school systems were "hurting" the results of school test results. Poor schools have a tendency to limit the number of families who wish to relocate in a community. In this case people were fleeing the failed city school systems to a system that even though it was beginning to fail was better than the city schools left behind. The county schools therefore only appeared attractive to poor socio-economic and racial minority families.

As a result, the political forces had to find a way to mask the deterioration of the local school's performance so that other demographic groups would also consider moving into the community. The political survival of local political leaders depended on their ability to recruit citizens likely to to accept the new academies at face value without the negative history. The needed Shoring-up action was to create a new perception of school quality by first renaming the schools and calling them "academies". The maneuver to rename basically destroyed the history of the "old schools". New schools meant a new history to write. Old higher test scores no longer existed for schools in the community. You can't get deteriorating scores if the former higher base score simply goes away.

A second issue to arise was political pressure from community leaders with new coalitions of support from new community minorities. They sought to "re-norm" the school testing methods to be more attuned to the new population. Translation, dumb it down. This did nothing but make people feel better. The schools true performance was masked by political leaders who were now facing the new realities of a potential power shift toward minority groups and doing what ever it takes to retain power for as long as possible in a new emerging political environment.

The declining schools and all that it effected had forced additional political action as opposed to real problem solving. As a consequence, more Shoring-up activity was instituted. The course that is taken will be directly effected by the level and intensity of the tension and disequilibrium. The presence of the new or prolonged community tension and perceived potential power disequilibrium caused the political leadership to engage in activity based on certain current situational expectations from constituents. In short the demands to "fix it" but don't hurt me in the process echoed in the ears of the political leadership. It did not take a seasoned politician to understand that political longevity was becoming severely limited. Politicians found grounds for accommodation to garner short term support. In several cases it was to insure support for higher office.

The Shoring-up actions taken by these political leaders was never directed at cause and effect of problems within the system for an important reason. The true solutions are not politically viable. To pursue any real long lasting solution is a political death wish for anyone wishing to remain in power. In most cases such solutions are now not politically correct and they are likely to cost a great deal and take a long time. We will revisit our communities at a later time to see how implementation of systems knowledge and defenses against politicians seeking to "Shore –up' their own positions of power allows the citizen activist to become a powerful force with the true power to address social problems in the political context.

Knowing What Needs to be Changed

Any attempt to intervene in, or divert the community/political system is an attempt at changing outcomes generated by that system. This requires not only knowing what really needs to be changed to address the key or underlying problems faced, but also eventually knowing how to make those changes.

Understanding the change process is the first step to initiating change. Attacking current system outcomes successfully is an exercise in problem solving and is a basic skill needed by the community and political activist. The intervention of strategic actions to implement change is the process of a planned move from one state of being to another more desirable situation. This is the movement from problem to problem solution.

The beginning step is that of problem analysis. That sounds so simple but is amazingly tricky. Quite often we are not in a position to view the entire playing field. That is why an understanding of the systems concept is critical. We need to know what and how all things are connected. An attempt to change one little element within a system, changes the entire system frequently into something that was never imagined. This change, if planned, controlled and understood; can be beneficial; but if our actions create "surprises" known as unintended consequences, we have failed to understand the workings of the community system. Our above examples of the community in a state of change are a good example of this situation.

The political process is one tied to the ability to exert influence and pressure. We need to understand the types and nature of pressures that can be brought to bear on politicians by citizens and conversely by politicians on those that attempt to challenge the status quo.

Assessing and diffusing sources of influence and power requires great skill and insight. We always have blind spots as to facts or insight into human behavior. We often are exposed to symptoms, mistaking them for the problem. The ability to recognize the real core problem, its source and power is essential for change strategies to work. Using the systems thinking approach means we have taken the time to observe and analyze the cause and effect relationships and have assessed the impact of any intervention.

Once the problem and its components are identified, a community leader can gain support from vital support groups. These groups will find value in changing the existing system or at least elements within the system that contribute to individual self interest. The perceived or actual power and influence of a new coalition will by its mere existence exert pressures within the system's processes to force reaction. This approach would be recognized by those who study organizational behavior as a planned change model. The heart of change process lies in defining the change problem. That is, what needs to occur before a desired future state can be achieved? An organized and directed process for getting from one condition to a desired other needs to be planned. To seek change for the sake of change without having a valid plan for what new system and processes will take the place of the old system is to invite disaster. This is an important distinction particularly in the political arena. Citizens groups have a tendency to only be able to describe what is wrong and all the accompanying evils. People who get things done plan for what they want. I think this is an important issue. Thinking in positive terms of what is to be, and not wasting energy and time bemoaning all the negatives. Ask any Cuban exile that when they supported the overthrow of Batista, if Fidel Castro was what they had in mind? Their energy was towards elimination of a negative without a clear plan of what the alternative should be. It matters little as to whether the change problem is large or small the process remains consistently the same. The movement from one state of being to another as a planned process is accomplished through the achievement of three goals. These are; transformation, reduction, and application.

The transformation goal is that of achieving recognition of the critical and essential differences between the current state and the desired future state.

The reduction goal is achieving the recognition of what must be "reduced" or eliminated and the processes or remedies required to bring the current state to the desired state. Perhaps a better term might be what strategy and tactical methods will move things to the desired state.

The third goal of application brings us to the "action plan" required to introduce and implement change using the strategies and tactics developed under the reduction goals.

Political Change is a WHAT, HOW and WHY Problem

At the very beginning of community discontent is the desire to effect some sort of positive change. Almost anybody and everybody effected by the current state of affairs can come to some consensus as to what the problem is, but the real problem becomes how to effect change. The "what" problem is defining what is it that needs to be changed?

Any type of diagnostic analysis is assumed since the desired outcome becomes the focus which forces the focus on what is the desired outcome. What does it look like and "what" changes are necessary to reach the desired condition. Let us not forget to also understand and anticipate the consequences of our actions within our community systems. Remember the archetype example given earlier. This challenge requires an identification of the processes that foster change within the current system. It is within this context that we seek to understand what will cause change. How do we get political leaders to act in the community interest when such behavior is in conflict with the political well being of the politician?

In our consideration of the "Why" question the ends and the means are relative notions, fluid, not absolute. The "why question", in this instance, becomes the push at explanation into the true relationships within the system. These often need to be traced to the final ends of change in order to understand systems and relationships. Consider the following string of Why questions which brings us to a true understanding of how the political system works in most communities.

1. Why do some political leaders appear to be non-responsive to public need?
   Because there is not a compelling reason to respond.
2. Why would a politician not be compelled to respond to constituents needs?
   Because they only serve a special interest minority with political clout.
3. Why do they only serve special interest?
   Because special interest control the fate of political leaders.

4. Why do special interests control the fate of political leaders?
    Because they control the resources of political power.
5. Why do they control resources for political control?
    Because the average citizen has abdicated responsibility
6. Why have they "dropped" out?
    Because the special interest have built power to steer political action, create alliances that control money, and access to media and votes.
7. Why do they create alliances that control money and access to media?
    Because political leaders want or need money and access to media.
8. Why do they seek money and media access?
    Because such access insures the ability to garner votes to stay in power.
9. Why do they get votes from special interest groups?
    Quid pro quo.
10. Why should I care?
    Because without your ability to offer something of value you get nothing of value.

The why question, allows us to formulate what needs to be accomplished. In this case it demonstrates that any group seeking change must first find a compelling reason for change to be initiated by a politician. The ultimate WHY should he do something for you if you can not deny him power, office, money or the ability to eliminate or divert these resources. Why questions are typically asked by people with no direct responsibility for the decisions or results. Once they are moved to the center of change activity, the questions quickly revert to "What" and "How".

CHAPTER

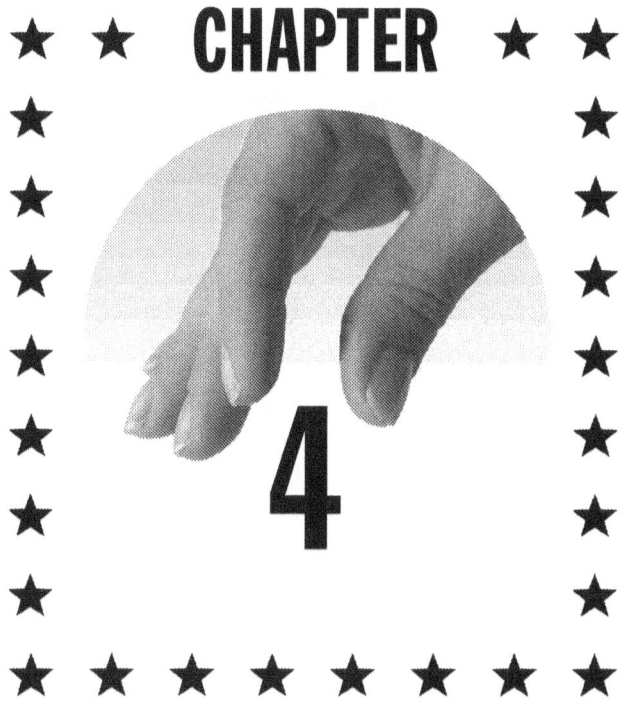

4

Politicians Think Differently

Chapter 4

Politicians Think Differently

The ability to influence, control, or threaten the power of political leaders requires that we first understand the nature and source of their power. This will lead us to an understanding of why and how political leadership is different from all other forms of leadership.

We begin this journey by taking an initial look at what leadership is and the essential differences found in the process of political leadership. As we will soon discover, political leadership is the subtle art of being a follower of political pressure.

Political leadership as leadership in general defies a common definition, but the concept of "we will know it when we see it", is simply not enough. One thing my experience tells me is that somehow political leadership and the rule under which it operates is different. Getting a handle on the how's of political power is something politicians do not openly discuss. From the view point of those who currently hold political leadership positions and the power that accompanies that position; there may be a vested interest in not revealing the workings of political power and leadership. To do so may render the politician and the process of obtaining and retaining political position more vulnerable than it is already. My search and attempt to definitively define what political leadership is, has been elusive. Definitions are as numerous as the multiple examples and settings that can be observed in various political systems.

However; citizen activists will be effected by political behaviors and political decisions. As such; we must understand the process by which political decisions are made. My research and self reflection demonstrates clearly that political leadership offers a unique and differentiated form of leadership and decision processes from almost any other socio-cultural organizational form. As a process, political leadership may be the best example of the servant leadership model where the leader is the follower of public opinion and the power of special interest groups.

Having an understanding of how the process of obtaining political influence and clout works, can only enhance the effectiveness of individual citizens and groups in their interaction with government bureaucrats or elected officials. Few of us truly recognize and understand, that we the people, whether as an individual with resources, or a citizen's group, hold the ultimate control of who is granted access to the power bestowed to political leaders.

When citizens understand the true workings of political systems and the use of proper interventions, then we can control our own destiny. More importantly we can better control our own politicians. I would argue that only those who have discovered the secrets of political life have any chance of directing the actions of politicians. When we have opposing groups with equal knowledge of the process, the spoils of political victory will go to the best organizers of power bases.

The novice has no chance in this game. My real purpose is not to educate the already engaged but to attract the novice and arm them with the tools to become a political force. Such an understanding may give those who choose to be involved in the development of public policy the insights necessary to effect political decision making.

The first reality we need to recognize is that to this point most citizens willingly abdicate this power for the seemingly safe confines of non-involvement. While ninety percent of the population seeks conflict avoidance, the other ten percent of the population has learned how to get their way and how to manipulate the lives of the rest of us for their own gain.

Demonstrations of political leadership more often than not will evoke both passionate opposition and passionate support within this self selected ten percent of adult activists. This group will determine public policy on any issue. If this fact is suddenly sobering to you, then the observations and dissection of political leadership that follows should be of vital interest to you.

If we examine the acquisition and holding of political power, we can conclude that it is the art of understanding which way the wind blows. It is how to gain support and strength-through the fickle will of opposing factions, each of which are competing for the exclusive use of society's resources. This of course all happens while the rest of the ninety percent bitch and moan their fate and the poor performance of the political power elite in addressing the needs of society.

Our attempts to describe and define the complex process of leadership makes it seem more orderly than it is. (Gardner.1990) Political process seems to work well in chaos. The fact that ninety percent of the population is disengaged from the political process for the most part allows for a majority of activists to play the game for political control and to define the issues. The American political system in its current incarnation depends on the maintenance of some chaos created for the ninety percent to keep them disengaged. It is this chaos that politicians depend upon to discourage the participation in the political process except by the ten percent. As we will discover in later chapters, order and harmony are not compatible in the long term with the political process. If we are to be effective as political change agents, then we must not only understand the chaos; we must become comfortable in the chaos and learn to use it for our own benefit.

For the average citizen, the topic of leadership and the workings of government hold little interest. It is something to be left to others to ponder. I believe that the lack of interest in the workings and acquisition of power and leadership positions by the average citizen, has contributed to the lack of any real focus on what is political leadership, or the processes that are engaged to gain and hold these positions.

Most people with whom I have talked, and supported by other studies, would at least agree that leadership in any arena is a Process of persuasion. This is a situation where individuals or groups are induced to pursue the vision and objectives of the leader (Ireh and Bailey. 1999). Others conclude that leadership is a combination of skills and aptitudes and situation (Bolman & Deal, 1991; Fieldler & Chemers, 1974; Stogdill, 1948). Both these positions and observation would suggest to me to be the essence of political activity.

In defining political leadership, there are two common elements that appear to be universal. The first, leadership does not occur in a vacuum since a leader must have followers and secondly, leadership has to do with the accomplishments of goals and objectives. The method or style seems to be secondary. Some writers would argue that one leadership style is appropriate for all circumstances (Blake & Mouton, 1994); others contend that different circumstances demand a difference in leadership styles (Hersey & Blanchard, 1988). This most certainly is the case in political environments and probably contributes to the impression by the non-initiated that most political leaders change positions and approaches with which way the wind blows. From the point of view of the political leader, this is how they seek and stay in power.

In my attempt to understand the idiosyncrasies of political leadership, I have conducted a diligent search for agreement upon what constitutes the basis of leadership and made the findings an integral part of my political decision model. Additionally, I examined the behaviors associated with the exercising of leadership and power along with the behaviors associated with the acquisition and retention of that power. I believe these elements represent a universal core of basic elements needed for successful political leadership. In doing so, I have also revealed the "Achilles Heel" of the politician that is useful to those who wish to change, divert or prop up a political position.

The process model offered is viewed from the vantage point of political leaders. This point of view is important in that any attempt to influence political action must be understood by how it is viewed or interpreted by the leader from whom action is sought.

I think it is constructive to examine some examples of various styles of political leadership. Even though these examples appear to be very different at first, some universal truths begin to emerge. I offer the following examples for your consideration; Mahatma Gandhi, Martin Luther King, Jr., John F. Kennedy and Ronald Reagan are persons who raised to significant political leadership positions. This is a rather diverse group on the surface, but I see three unifying behaviors that link these leaders.

The first is an unshakable belief in something. The second is a passion to promote, protect and persuade others of that belief. The third, is translating that belief into a vision for the future. Through these examples we can see how leadership plays a critical role in attempts to adjust or change human social-political systems. For King, it was a vision of one American that was given its focus in his "I have a dream" speech. For Kennedy it was a vision of a strong America in the face of the Soviet threat and his launching of the space program to put men on the moon. Reagan's vision of a united Europe and the fall of the Soviet Union was the core of his presidency. For

Gandhi, it was life experiences and situations that transform him from lawyer to world leader of a non-violent revolution that liberated India from British control. (Burns, 1978.p 107)

Besides understanding the power of the commitment and attachment these leaders had with their own visions of what they wanted to obtain; think of the power certain individuals and groups would have or had on these leaders if they were able to become potential obstacles to that vision or on the other hand could help deliver the vision to a reality.

In influencing or changing the political system, or at least diverting it, the activist needs to either finds ways to support or disrupt the political quest of a vision. The power and commitment to a vision is both the political strength and the Achilles heel of any political leader. It is this aspect of political leadership that contributes to its uniqueness from other forms of leadership.

Political leadership is distinctly different from management and political leadership is different from all other forms of leadership. Political leaders are in essence "slaves" to the "leader as follower model" in that their ability to be a political leader is dependent upon the ability to follow the will of the majority of the politically active population or inspire such acceptance of a vision from the same primary group.

Some politicians also exhibit the skill of management. Typical management activity can and does take direct action to deal with the solution of issues. In most cases in business the decisions and solutions selected are not dependent upon a democratic process of majority rule. In the manager's domain, the main objective is the efficiency of an organization. The political manager/leader does not have this luxury.

The difference between managing and leadership is important to distinguish. While leaders manage and managers lead they are not synonymous (Bass. 1981). Even though these activities overlap, each entails unique activities. The manager's role is enmeshed in the function of management, namely planning, organizing, directing, and controlling. In the political process, the role of manager falls to the bureaucracy that implements political programs.

Leadership, particularly social and political leadership, is a process of creating a common vision and the use of assertive persuasion.

I believe that an essential element of social and political leadership is the total passion to the vision. Leadership, and the power of leadership, is derived from the followers that have bought into the vision of the leader, not the position that the leader may hold. This element is important to remember. It will be reintroduced in later chapters when the tools that citizens can utilize to control political and social issues are examined. Societal and social institutional leadership is broadly intended to effect change (Burns.1980, p.434). Leaders seek to inspire, provide emotional support and deal with the interpersonal aspects of managing (Bass, 1981).

The concept of power for managers is derived from the position they hold or in combination to power derived from some special expertise. While the average citizen may view the power of the politician as linked to the office they hold, we will provide insight that demonstrates that the power truly is derived from the people and as such "we the people" hold the key to control. Burns refers to leadership as the "authoritative allocation of values" that are considered the legitimate use of power.

For the political leader, the exercising of this power is not without consequences. If considered inappropriate or in conflict with the vision, followers may abandon the leader in favor of another that adheres to the vision. This behavior, in no small part, accounts for political party defections when the message coming from the political leader is one of negativism in which one asserts the "against position" without offering a competing positive vision.

Successful political leadership is a unique blending of individual characteristics and traits, situation, opportunity and willingness of leader and followers. (Yukl, June 1989, p274) As we progress in our analysis into the elements of political power it will become clear that those who hold political leadership and seek the retention of power will vigorously protect and defend it at almost any cost.

They will use both followers and opposition in anyway to protect power and to protect their core values that constitute the political vision. This construct is central in our understanding of political leaders and the process of gaining their favor and support for our causes.

The Transformational Leader versus the Political Transaction Leader

When citizens seek to make change they assume the role of transformational leader. Simply put, you are seeking to change something that is attuned to your vision of how things ought to be. The political leader on the other hand, is a transactional leader with a vested interest in the status quo. This means that the political animal is more interested in a process which focuses on the concept of exchange of favors.

The transitional approach seeks an end game with value. For the politician, this is a pay as you go game. This may seem a little mercenary to the causal observer. After all, didn't this same politician at the beginning of his quest in seeking office offer his followers some transformational vision for their support? Yes he did, and probably delivered that promise and will work like hell to keep things the way they got transformed. As such, the cycle of power seeking and power shoring-up continues.

Below I have created my model of political actions as an attempt to illustrate the process undertaken by politicians in determining how to act when confronted with a political issue.

This can be particularly instructive when considering why political issues are sometimes simply not addressed or at other time acted upon quickly. The bottom line for the politician is that if he gets it wrong, he faces at the least political embarrassment and at the most political defeat.

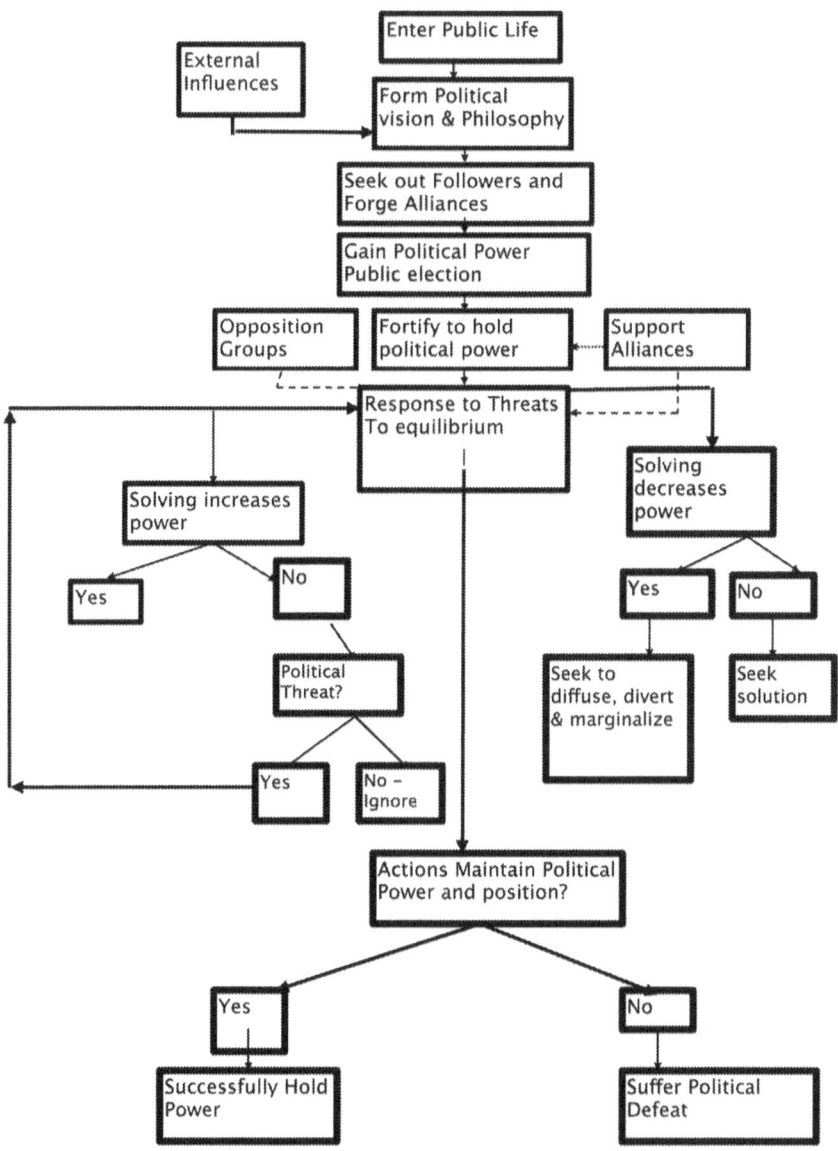

The Model of Political Actions

The process model above can be more fully appreciated with a simple explanation of the flow of event in a politician's life. First, people who enter political life as I said in the introduction usually do so for honorable perhaps even altruistic reasons. Success in entering the arena is tied to the aspiring politician's ability to inspire a group of followers, financial and political backers to buy in to a political vision and a political philosophy. If successful, the politician's initial followers become evangelist for the vision and the new political philosophy hopefully culminating in the election of the aspirant to elected office.

However, once in office several phenomenon begin to take place. The first and almost inescapable is the fact that the newly elected official really likes all the attention and begins to understand and seek the perks of power. The second thing that takes place is that those groups of activist that paved the way to elected office want political favors in return. Even other groups that were not the initial supporters will seek recognition and favor from the new politician.

Pretty soon the politician is confronted with demands from competing groups. It is at this point that the politician is forced into "typical" political behavior of not being primarily concerned with solving problems but protecting themselves from political fallout caused by the emergence of some political disequilibrium. He is forced in some cases to take sides, to ignore other factions while embracing still others. When forced to find a balance between opposing factions, the politician finds ways to "Shore-up: the support and power from all sides for his own advantage and protection. A major portion of our remaining discussion will be devoted to recognizing this Shoring-Up behavior so that it is not mistaken for any positive political action that benefits anyone other than the politician.

A key in getting ones social-political issue within the radar of the politician or bureaucrat is to know where you and your issue fall within the Model's decision criteria. If favorable, then positive action is almost guaranteed. However, if your issue falls into the unimportant sector of the decision process, then it is imperative that you know that and recognize that some sort of action is required to create disequilibrium in the political environment.

The Art of Political Decisions and Non-Decisions

As is suggested in the above model and explanation, politicians only make positive political decisions when the positive action enhances or secures their own personal position.

If the required decision threatens their position or most likely does nothing for them; a positive decision is not going to happen. Period! All other actions that "simulate" political action are to be classified as "Shoring-up" activities. We will look at the elements and the process of this unique political behavior below.

When reflecting on the political process, as practiced by the American politician, I am reminded of a line in a Woody Allan movie, when Allen's character is asked the question; "Do you think sex is dirty?" Allen responded with "if it's done right." A funny line for sure but within its premise is a basic truth about politics.

Politics if done right is messy; it's unpredictable and sometimes dirty. Some political scientists have referred to it as chaotic and the ultimate social maze (Stone, 2002). Yet it is through this chaos that western civilization functions, grows and even survives by way of the political process.

To understand the causes and types of behavior in which political players and democratic societies engage is to understand ourselves as individuals and as a society. The bottom line is that as independent social or political groups, we have virtually no chance for the success of our ideals or social visions without an understanding of the process and practice of political non-decision making.

Political decision making or in most cases non-decision making is interesting in a number of ways but particularly interesting that in some vague way the general populace views the process as corrupt and unseemly. Stone (2002. p.376) even suggests that Americans would rather replace the entire process with rational decision making.

The fact is, if you understand the system, it is already rational. The average citizen needs to see and understand that rationality in terms of knowing the rules for how the system works.

In addition, you need to know not only the rules, but what game you are playing. The art of getting one's way is the essences of the political process. It is my intention to arm community activists and the average citizen with the tools and the armor of political process for defending and defeating deliberate non-decisions in order to get your political way.

This will be done through the in-depth look at a section of my Political Action Model to be called "Political Shoring-up." Shoring up behaviors are the politician's responsive actions to impending political disequilibrium or disruption.

While targeted toward the context of community, state and national political systems, the conceptual model of Shoring-up is useful within any organization that has a political environment-that is basically all organizations.

My "Shoring-up" political behavior model demonstrates that political decision making is calculated for best personal political gain, it is planned to deliver the least to opponents and the most to supporters. It is highly rational in that it gives the political leader and office holder the opportunity to secure power and the retention of office. Its' rationality is demonstrated as a response to how society forces an approach to political decision making that seeks immediate action and generally forces the taking of sides. As one politicians said to me;" It is a process of finding and using wedge issues to break and beat the opposition." Political leadership and the holding of power are dependent upon the politician's ability to calculate consequences and to estimate the ability of special interest groups to exert influence at the ballot box. As this rational model demands, there are facts underlying all situations and political decisions. Politics may be energized by emotion but its decisions are cold hard calculation weighing the consequences as to how actions could lead to a threat to power.

Political reasoning and decisions are always conducted as part of that struggle between conflicting groups, goals and keeping power. Politics and the political process is the ultimate reality show. The stakes are high, there are winners and losers. I know that this may come as a shock to those who believe in the morality of political correctness where there can be no losers in that strange fantasy land where we are all always winners. Get over it, or condemn yourself to the abyss of the politically naïve or as I prefer to say, "Welcome to the ninety percent that doesn't have a clue."

Political process is designed to control the immediate environment and situation which makes long term solutions very difficult. Political shoring-up behavior is a behavior geared for political survival. The survival instinct in a politician is an important attribute if they are to be successful as a political leader. Political reason and decision making is a process of persuasion. Sometimes this is gentle in nature but is just as likely to fall into the hardball quid pro quo world of political power and favors. It is a process of winning the hearts and minds of the populace so that some greater vision can be pursued.

Not all political behavior around decision making is Shoring-up. Political leaders do in fact seek and pursue real solutions to the problems of their constituencies. The dichotomy between Shoring-up and attempts at solving a real problem lies in the benefits of solving the problem.

My experience and observations as a political operative interacting with numerous politicians over the years is that if the solution of a problem works to enhance the image of the political leader or the solution contributes towards the political vision then the politicians will move mountains to fix the issue.

On the other hand, If the solving the issue in anyway threatens the political vision or the politician's position with his support base, than Shoring-up is embraced.

★ ★ CHAPTER ★ ★

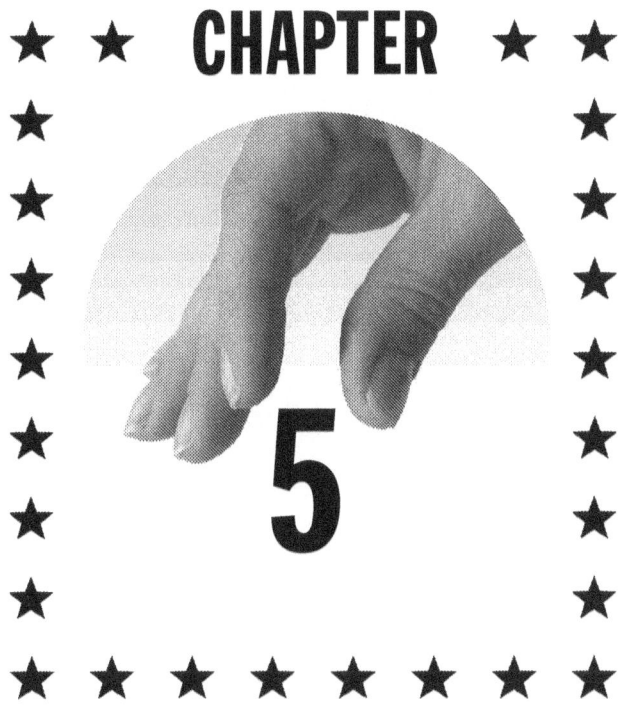

5

Shoring-up, Political Self Preservation

Chapter 5

Shoring-up, Political Self Preservation

It is now the appropriate time to explore political decision making and actions in context from the point of view of those who make political decisions. It is first important to state right up front- political decisions are always made in light of political survival and protection of the core ideology of the office holder and their political party.

The Shoring-up model is an articulation and integration of observations, ideas, behaviors strategies and tactical applications that have emerged from countless hours of research utilizing methods of observation, interviewing and engaging in the process that has allowed me to discover the essence of political decision making. This essence can be boiled down to the concept of the core variable-Shoring-up- which concisely demonstrates how political leaders act when confronted with challenges that potentially threaten their status or power. Confronted with such situations, politicians begin a set of behaviors that follows a precise pattern that is calculated, formalized and prescriptive for the sole purpose of eliminating or marginalizing opponents that pose any threat. The term shoring up or to shore up ones position is a concept that most of us have heard. What is unique in this study is that for the first time the process of the behavior is dissected and analyzed in a manner that allows for the development of strategy and tactical approaches for dealing with the Shoring-up behaviors that will most certainly arise when potential confrontation occurs caused by citizens groups seeking to influence the political process.

The Shoring-up model is significant, in that; it for the first time identifies behaviors and patterns in political decision processes that lies somewhere in-between popular concepts of Satisficing behaviors and the variety of approaches used in strategic decision making. This new space has to this point in time not been enumerated in the management or political science literature.

Shoring-up behaviors operate in a sequential and recursive pattern of threat identification leading to the strategies and tactics to render such threats harmless. Interview data would suggest that Shoring-up is at times both a conscious and unconscious reflexive response by political leaders.

As will be further illuminated more extensively in later chapters, the basis for Shoring-up behaviors is rooted in the politician's core beliefs and the espoused visions. This is their political philosophy. My model identifies this philosophical development process as "Forging".

Just as the strength of steel is forged in the blast furnace, it is "Forging" that molds and casts these sets of beliefs and vision in which all political decisions are made. For the political leader, the core philosophy must be protected through shoring-up behaviors. If in the perception of the politician, he believes that a threats exist, then appropriate defenses will be implemented.

The successful seeking and the retention of political power and elected office often hinges on the ability of the politician and those around him to sense threats that have the potential to compromise or divide the political powerbase.

Political action and decision making takes on the role of placing a protective shell around the political leader to keep in tact the political philosophy and the agenda that accompanies the central vision. The successful political leader is one that continuously "feels" the political environment. I refer to this process as "Sensing".

The "Sensing" stage of Shoring-up identifies the conditions of tension, political disequilibrium and potential threats of derailment to the vision. The sensing stage is where political disruptions are at a level to become noticed. A shift or unexpected change in this level can lead to conditions that insure Shoring-up behaviors given that the threat is assessed as dangerous.

The process of Political Shoring-up identifies the next sequential stage as that of "Reacting" to the changes in the political environment that offer the potential for a threat to the vision and political power. The behavioral actions that are found in "Reacting" are scanning, assessing, and diffusing.

Each of these actions has a distinct function. "Scanning" is the process of monitoring the political environment this is done on a constant basis. Typical scans include monitoring the economic, social-cultural, legal and regulatory environments for indications that any change may have either a positive or negative impact on the reaching of the vision.

This is a more targeted and purposeful look at the environment versus what the theory identifies in the Sensing stage. The difference lies in that scanning is a deliberate and organized activity whereas; sensing is triggered by a perceptual change by the politician in the environment caused by deliberate actions or reaction from opposition groups.

The "Assessing" activity is more or less the evaluation of the information derived from the Scanning process. The assessment will allow the political leader to select one of three strategies to address information from the scan. The strategies are:

1. To engage in overt offensive mode behaviors to address an either positive or negative issue.
2. Take a defensive mode to protect from attack by the opposition.
3. Decide that no action is necessary.

The choice of strategy will be tied to what is believed to be necessary to maintain the political equilibrium to hold off threats to political power.

"Diffusing" is a process to relieve political pressure brought about by opposition groups. The activity-Shoring-up- is launched if an action is required to re-establish equilibrium. In theory the process of Shoring-up moves to the action strategy to eliminate threats. The object of Diffusing is to first lower or eliminate the built up political tension. Once tension has been lessened, the strategy move to find methods that will restore a state of equilibrium and make the initial attempts to return to the vision.

Once the strategies are deployed to re-establish political control, it is vital that the political leaders quickly return to an environment that is as close as possible to the original state of equilibrium.

This stage of the process has been identified as the "Normalizing" stage. It is in this stage of Shoring-up that all players from both the opposition and the internal support groups must be brought to their original positions of acceptance. This is accomplished through the use of "justifying" strategies as will be detailed in later chapters.

Additionally, the politician must work at reinforcing his support through the use of rewards and punishment for supporters and any who tried to oppose the mission and vision. The politician will then move to consolidate power and if possible find support from the ranks of the defeated in order to solidify and expand the support base.

This is the political process of Shoring-up. For the political player, it is a natural way of life. It is easily observable. It tends to be a process that is not turned on and off as needed but a continuous and recursive process.

In-depth Look of Shoring up Behaviors

In any attempt to seek or gain political advantage, it is vital that the political behavior or Shoring-up be recognized and understood. To not recognize the behavior is to be lulled into the belief that your concerns are being addressed when they may not be. Without such an understanding, opposition groups or groups that holds no political clout can not expect to effect a change in the status quo while it remains in a political equilibrium.

Stages of Shoring-Up

As citizens having been "Shored-up" against and not really knowing it, the act is mostly invisible to us. In truth the process has a behavioral base found at the very beginning of one political career. As such, we need to understand the core values and ultimate goals of politicians and political movements to understand why and how their particular Shoring-up behavior is based.

The four stages in the Shoring-up process were identified above. Again these stages are; the Forging stage, the Sensing stage, the Reacting stage, and the Normalizing stage. Each of these is examined in the following pages. Some might question the need to know this. A logical question might be, how will this help me address community social issues? The answer lies in that you must know how the politician is viewing the scene and what makes them vulnerable. It is simply important to understand this process in order to effect change. Knowing what to look for will put you on equal footing with the professional manipulators of public policy.

How Politicians Build and Hold Power

The process of building a political power base requires the politician to find or in my terms "forge" willing followers of the espoused political philosophy and vision.

The Forging stage sets the parameters and conditions under which Shoring-up takes place. At its core, Forging identifies what is to be protected by the Shoring-up process. Forging has four basic properties. These are visioning, seeking, pledging, and pleading. These establish the political base and the political promise that begins the journey of political leadership. In some aspects it is the beginnings of group formation and has some similarities to the forming, storming and norming stages of group dynamics (Tuchman, 1965).

Visioning -Political Promise

Visioning is a distinct process that is separate and apart from planning. Planning asks participants to create goals and objectives and devise a plan of action to meet these objectives within the resources available. The process selects the most effective and efficient manner to reach the goals. Visioning, on the other hand, requires leaders to consider what a community, city, company, or any other organization could be at a future date, even though the resources do not currently exist to make this dream happen. As part of the political visioning process, political leaders create an action plan to attract followers and other resources that will facilitate the implementation of a program to accomplish their vision for the community they serve. In his presidential nomination speech, John Kerry offered his vision for America in the very first sentence of the delivery as follows; "My fellow Americans: we are here tonight united in one simple purpose: to make America stronger at home and respected in the world." This sets forth the vision of Democratic presidential candidate, Kerry, and will be the basis for his campaign's strategy and targets a broader support base.

While the differences in approach may seem pedantic, they are substantive in that the visioning process makes participants look beyond existing resources and methods to try to find new roles for the political community and its' resources by building on current strengths (Walzer, 1996, p. 13). According to a former county elected official, visioning tends to be associated with or about protecting or improving quality of life issues that have impact on the follower group.

According to several Maryland politicians and my own experiences as a political candidate, current and would be political leaders tend to be oriented toward one of two approaches to visioning. These are the *ideological* approach and the *pragmatic* approach. The ideological approach is tied to a politicians deeply held set of beliefs that structure the totality of thought and actions. Followers of such political leaders tend to also hold those same beliefs and offer little to no tolerance for any deviation by the leader from the vision that uses the ideology as its core. Examples of such leaders might include Ronald Reagan, Gandhi, and George W. Bush. Each exhibited a strong sense of their own morality and beliefs in the visions they offered. They let their core values set the tone and direction of the vision. These politicians let the core values dictate how to approach problems.

The pragmatic approach ties a vision of a collective greater good. This approach may cause the leader who offers a pragmatic vision to suspend or subordinate core beliefs in favor of an approach that seeks to capture the support of a more eclectic following. We can find examples such as politicians who have had to deal with the conflict in personal values and greater public interest. Many politicians wrestle with a personal conviction against abortion, but support abortion rights.

Examples of pragmatic visionary leaders would include

Bill Clinton, Jimmy Carter and Gerald Ford. Each of them set a mission to handle the problems of the day and offered a vision of a better America based on handling specific problems. Failure to keep opposition in check results in opposition forming alliances and partnering to gain political power and derailing the vision. "To grasp and hold a vision", observed Ronald Reagan, "that is the very essence of successful leadership..." (Heilbrunn, 1994, p. 65)

Seeking the Pillars of Support

If leadership consists of getting things accomplished through others, then those "others" are critical to the leader's effectiveness. The seeking and finding of followers that accept the same vision is critical. Having found a core constituency, political leaders empower their followers to promote the vision. Empowerment implies that followers are central to the organization, rather than tangential to it. They become the evangelists. Empowered followers believe that they make a difference and their actions have significance and meaning.

They have discretion in what they do, but are also accountable for their actions (Rosenbach & Taylor, 1998, p. 86). Political leaders cannot lead without empowered followers. The importance of the role of follower cannot be under estimated, "...effective leadership depends on a context of followership in which people are related meaningfully to their work [cause]. Otherwise, a leader's 'vision' cannot motivate anyone or coalesce activity" (Krantz, 1990, p. 55). Likewise, political leaders instinctively seek to expand their following from the initial core group of followers. Followers in the political context are seen as active, not passive; politics is a contact sport that requires an active role as followers themselves engage in leadership, not just in followership. Leadership involves more than leaders getting followers to carry out leaders' wishes; that is, motivating followers as does a transactional or charismatic leader (Rosenbach & Taylor, 1998).

Political leaders seek to form coalitions with other individuals, groups, institutions, agencies, and collectives for the purpose of supporting a common shared community vision. For the political leader seeking to retain power and influence and indeed his office, these associations may at times necessarily involve compromise and creative infidelity to one's own group or tradition as one accepts limited amounts of contamination on behalf of keeping political equilibrium and moving towards the perfection of the vision (Holland, 1999).

Pledging (the political promise)

A political vision becomes the basis for political campaigns and the political focus of public policy initiatives. It becomes the promise in exchange for support from the constituent groups. This is clearly demonstrated in the nomination acceptance speech given by Senator John Kerry at the 2004 Democratic National Convention in Boston. His pledge was given as follows:

"We have it in our power to change the world again, but only if we're true to our ideals [the vision]...and that starts by telling the truth to the American people. That is my first pledge to you tonight. As President, I will restore trust and credibility to the White House."

Pledging tends to take one of two forms depending on whether the politician is the office holder or is seeking to replace the incumbent. An incumbent is dependent upon his base supporters who are also guardians of the vision offered by the political leader. As such, the incumbent's pledging is in the form of pledges to "stay the course" and to deliver on political promises.

A political challenger on the other hand, is forced to make two pledges. The first is in the form of an attack on the office holder's vision or in his ability to deliver on the vision. Second, the challenger must articulate either a new vision that will captivate a formidable following or offer a plan to achieve the former vision in some way better than the incumbent. In a political party primary contest where general core principles prevail, the latter is usually the case.

Pledging is in essence the political contract between the political leader and their followers. The pledge identifies what the political leader will do and say on their behalf in exchange for their votes and support. It is this contract to which followers will hold politicians accountable for their actions and breeches of the contract.

Incumbents are forced to alter their pledging process to first illuminate their record, to remind the political base that they defended the vision and mission. The incumbent additionally then is required restate their commitment to the vision and state the future agenda as the extension of the original pledge.

Pleading for the Quid pro Quo

The act of pleading is the asking for support given that the pledge or contract offer has been accepted. At this stage the pleading is very specific. It simply and directly asks for votes, volunteers and dollars. Additionally, it is the call to action. The call asks volunteers to become the evangelist for the cause and to organize the political campaign. This call to action and a plea for votes was again demonstrated in the acceptance speech of presidential candidate John Kerry. "Never has there been a more urgent moment for Americans to step up and define ourselves. I will work my heart out. But, my fellow citizens, the outcome is in your hands more than mine."

It is in this pleading phase that the organizers also engage in activities such as voter registration in tight precincts. This process will also seek the support of a wider audience through the use of public endorsements by special interest groups such as labor unions and or business associations. Through this activity, the pleading process takes on a multiplier factor that expands the opportunities for votes, volunteers and fund raising.

The results of federal elections and to some extent state elections are largely due to the political activity and education programs of the labor movement. The AFL-CIO's political arm, COPE, at every level, functions effectively in terms of funding, manpower, communications, registration and get out-the-vote apparatus, and precinct-level organization. (Caddy, 1974)

For the incumbent, Pleading is directed at the core support groups suggesting that their continued preferred status of being "in" is dependent upon their willingness to pay the price to retain the influence and power.

CHAPTER

6

Are You Perceived to be a Threat?

Chapter 6

Are You Perceived to be a Threat?

A critical stage in the Shoring Up process is the ability to develop a method that identifies political danger. I refer to this step as the "sensing" stage. Perhaps a politician's greatest need and their best demonstrations of political acumen is knowing when the winds of public opinion changes direction. Without this ability the prospects of gaining and retaining political power is greatly diminished. This leads us to a discussion of "sensing".

During the Sensing stage, the three conditions of "tension," "disequilibrium," and the threat of "derailment" could surface for the politician which will cause Shoring-up behaviors to begin. These conditions are forces that try to eliminate or neutralize cooperation or seek to change the existing political dynamic. In the political setting, according to a former county executive, cooperation and competition are equally important, because the political process will not work, will not move towards common visions, or even survive, without their presence.

Observation of the political process would indicate that the development of public policy involves the seeking of allies and building the cooperation necessary to compete with opposing factions. Whenever more than two sides of any issue emerge, alliances must be made with one side in order to have movement toward a resolution.

This was further demonstrated in the case study of the Hill Top and Lakeside communities in dealing with the issue of crime. On one hand, the politicians needed to respond to community outcries for more police protection and on the other hand be sensitive to the new racial composition of the community and the reaction to an increase in police presence by the racial minorities. By bringing community leaders from both groups together to develop a plan for decreasing crime that included joint community police patrols, a potential political problem was diverted.

It is in this stage that the political leader is alerted to the possibility of opposition, which if not addressed may lead to a threat to power, influence and the ability to achieve the results of the political vision. Cooperation is central to the political process, because it is essential for power. Cooperation is often a more effective form of subordination than coercion. Authority that depends solely on coercion cannot extend very far. Even prison guards, with seemingly all the resources stacked on their side, need the cooperation of inmates to "keep order" (Stone, 2002, p. 25). The conditions of this stage of Shoring-up, tension, disequilibrium and threat of derailment are forces that change the dynamic between cooperation and competition in political environments.

Condition of Tension

The condition of tension, in stage two of Shoring-up, occurs when individuals and groups are disenfranchised through the loss of political influence and power in some way. Increases in tension are generally derived from the perception of constituents that call into issue the ability of the leader's vision or agenda to deal with five basic areas. These are process, structure, effectiveness, resources, and competence (Matta, 1999).

Tension can emanate from both external groups or from internal turmoil of supporters. In general, these sources can lead to one of three types of tension, with several variations. These are: (1) Vision Conflict; which can arise from internal and external pressure, (2) Loss of Confidence in Leadership; which can arise from a change in core principles, a change in the vision, a lack of ability or trust, and the influence of outside events, and (3) Follower Indifference.

Vision Conflict

Vision conflict can originate from either external opposition groups or internal support groups. Types of vision conflict emanating from opposition groups may take the form of seeking to interfere in or break coalitions and seeking to assemble new opposition alliances to oppose the vision and leader. These opposition groups, with proper motivation, seek to derail the political leader by finding ways to disrupt the current mission or vision. In an effort to gain political influence and to change the agenda or even dislodge the incumbent, opposition groups will develop strategic alliances with other groups who also wish to derail or change the agenda. The ultimate goal is to replace the current power holder or change the mission. This threat to the vision creates conflict within the group, which in turn, introduces a state of tension.

Vision conflict can also be a product of internal group conflict. The types of conflict may be a perceived breach in the ideology or a fractioning of the support base.

A breach is brought on by a political leader where the core group of followers stay with the vision, but the developer of the vision for some reason feels compelled to either augment the vision or abandon the vision altogether. In this case, supporters will seek to compel the leader to return to the vision and its' core principles through the threat of the withdrawal of support in the future.

Fractioning on the other hand, seems to be the product of some supporters not universally in favor of holding the leader to the core values of the vision. This is demonstrated in the "my guy, right or wrong" approach. We can see this being played out in the 2004 presidential election where both candidates have departed from the core ideology and vision of their political parties leaving fractures in their supporter base. George W. Bush has seemingly abandoned the conservative concept of limited government. Kerry has, against the wishes of the liberal core of his party, vowed to stay the course in the war against Iraq. In spite of the ideology conflict, there is little indication that the party faithful will switch sides or withhold support.

Loss of Confidence in Leadership

The next source of political tension is a demonstration that there has been a loss of confidence in leadership. Data from my observations over the years and discussions with a variety of political pundits suggest that this occurs one or a combination of four ways: first, a change of core principles; second, a change of vision; third, a lack of ability and or trust; and fourth, an unexpected outside action or event. Examples from national politics are offered later in this section.

Influence works not simply by putting one individual under the figurative spell of another, but also in ways that lead to curious phenomena of collective behavior. "Bandwagon effects" in elections happen when a candidate's initial lead causes people to support him or her because they want to be on board with a winner…(but) people's choice is conditional (Stone, 2002, p. 24).

Change of core principles

Political groups are held together by a belief and value system as any other group, perhaps more intensely. Tension can emerge if it is perceived that the leader has changed or abandoned any of the core values that support the overall vision. The reverse variation of this is also possible when the followers, for various reasons, selectively abandon core principles that are essential elements of the leader's vision.

If done by small numbers of members, the group and leader will adopt strategies that either bring the offenders back in line or expel them from the group. This seems to be the role played by religious leaders with followers in a constant effort to keep them on task of seeing the vision and adhering to the core beliefs. Tension can emerge, not only from political rivals outside the politicians support groups, but can also arise within the political group if the leader seems to drift, augment, or abandon the mission in anyway without the consent of the group. George H.W. Bush, forty-first President of the United States, has been accused of abandoning the core principle of smaller government and no new taxes. A movement away from that principle punished him with the loss of the presidency to Bill Clinton.

Change of vision

Tension can emerge within the political group if a political leader abandons the core beliefs of his supporter groups. This sometimes is forced upon a political office holder when he finds himself at odds with the support group over a change in personal beliefs and philosophy. In this situation, I have seen leaders change political parties to find a better fit for the shift in vision. U.S. Senator Ben Lighthorse Campbell fell out of favor with the Democratic Party with his shift to more conservative view on welfare. Sensing that he could not win a Democratic re-nomination for the Senate, he switched to the Republican Party and won re-election. In Maryland, Democratic State Senator Frank Kelley, a devout Catholic, was ousted after more than twenty years in the Senate in his party's primary for failure to support a pro-choice piece of legislation. This was a decision based on his religious philosophy. In a conversation, Senator Kelley explained that his moral focus on abortion and his public stand on his moral political thinking were directly responsible for the fracture between the voters in the Democratic primary and himself.

Lack of ability and or trust

Tension can also rise if the political harmony is disrupted by the perception of a leader's inability to deal with the issues at hand or if an issue of trust arises. This has been demonstrated in the presidency of Richard Nixon, when the issue of trust and honesty drove him from office. Bill Clinton, constantly mired in ethical controversy, survived an impeachment, but his presidency will most likely be, rightly or wrongly, remembered and judged on his sexual appetite. Jimmy Carter's presidency was ultimately decided on the issue of ability. While widely thought of as a decent and honest man, he was accused as being a micro manager not capable of leadership, particularly in foreign affairs.

In observing community meetings, it became clear that the continuation of positive relationships and indeed continued support between community leaders and elected leaders, rested on the perceived competence of the county executive and the district councilman in addressing the crime and education issues.

The outside event

Another source for a lack of confidence in a political leader can be the product of an unplanned or unexpected outside event. The inability to handle such an occurrence to the satisfaction of supporters or to provide a basis to deflect criticism from opposition groups is tension producing and will most likely provide the fuel for Shoring-up behaviors. On the national scene, it is evident that the event of the terrorist attack on the World Trade Center was of such political magnitude that it changed the entire vision and political program of, not only a president, but also a nation.

The war on terrorism is in and of itself a form of Shoring-up. The political survival of the Bush administration may lie on the perception of supporters and opposition groups.

The power of an outside event can also be demonstrated in my observation of the county communities of Hill Top and Lakeside. Unexpectedly, rapid demographic changes to these communities caused county and state political leaders to take action to address crime increases and a falling real estate market.

During conversations on the Hill Top and Lakeside communities with the sitting county executive and several of his staff, concerns were expressed about how the county executive's inability to find a quick fix for the community problems without causing other charges of racial insensitivity would affect his newly announced run for Governor.

Follower and Voter Indifference

According to data derived from interviews with both elected politicians and community activists, the most dangerous and tension producing situations are seen in the case of supporter indifference. This situation occurs when political leadership fails to motivate and or inspire supporters.

This has the potential of allowing opposition groups the ability to gain power and control through the inaction of support groups. We often hear politicians talk about energizing the base. Failure to do so can cause defeat. According to a post-mortem analysis by the Republican National Committee, the conservative base of the Republican Party became indifferent to the candidacy of George H.W. Bush when he abandoned the core value of no new taxes. They did not vote against him and for Bill Clinton. They simply saw no difference between the candidates and stayed home on Election Day. That indifference combined with the third party candidacy of Ross Perot allowed Bill Clinton to win with a plurality rather than a majority vote.

Condition: Disequilibrium

"Tension" is a prerequisite for disequilibrium. When tension rises to a level that appears to the political leader as becoming an eminent threat to the vision agenda, disequilibrium comes into being. This state requires immediate and directed action either to enforce support group norms or to neutralize the threat from opposition groups. Disequilibrium is a state in which political pressure causes imbalance in the group dynamics, which can cause confusion, and resistance to political agendas. Situations that could create disequilibrium are numerous, but according to an interview with a high level political appointee; there are two basic sources for this disequilibrium. These are a change in the system equilibrium or a change in the process equilibrium.

System disequilibrium

The context for system disequilibrium is found in operating structures of human organization, such as communities or even political parties. The Structural functionalists; such as, Merton (1957) and Parsons (1968), demonstrated that the behavior of the group system and its' component individual parts is determined by the total system's needs and goals. Should those goals become less clear, for any reason, group focus, and commitment to the goal or political vision is endangered.

Data gathered at community meetings and interviews from the Hill Top and Lakeside communities indicate that issues such as school performance, poor economic conditions, zoning disputes, rising crime rates, and taxation are typical areas that can quickly and unexpectedly change, causing tension leading to system disequilibrium. As was demonstrated in the Hill Top community, a shift of attention to these kinds of issues, on the part of public leaders, can derail a community and its' leaders from the vision and political agenda, thus affecting current public policy. Latham (1956, p. 239) described public policy in terms of states of equilibrium.

"What may be called public policy is actually the equilibrium reached in the group struggle at any given moment, and it represents a balance which the contending factions or groups constantly strive to tip in their favor...Legislation referees the group struggle, ratifies the victories of successful coalition, and records the terms of surrenders, compromises, and conquest in the form of statutes".

Process disequilibrium

In the context of disequilibrium, the process refers to the manner in which individuals and groups get things done within the system. Group theory proposes that interaction among groups is a central element of the political process where individuals with common interests band together to press their demands on the political leadership (Dye, 2002, p. 21).

If the community or opposition group's demands are in conflict with the established political process or have the potential of diverting focus from the goals, a state of process disequilibrium emerges and forces the leader to deal with the imbalance. J.M. Burns (1978) has suggested that public and community conflicts may be sharper and more contentious because of the process of legal requirements for public officials to respond for clients that can exert pressure on them. Resolution is further challenged by a political climate that restricts an objective setting and the treatment of all factions in an evenhanded manner.

Political correctness is in many circumstances the element that shifts a harmonious situation to one of group conflict and into process disequilibrium. In modern western political society, pressure groups that set in motion the condition of disequilibrium can be found among the numerous voluntary associations, such as labor unions, trades associations, community associations and other reform groups that have some interest at stake in politics (De Grazia, 2004).

Not surprisingly, pressure-groups have grown in close relation to the various political party systems. Even when there are many non-party aligned groups or individuals, these interest groups are absorbed into the party system to be either in opposition to the leadership or to rally in support to protect the vision. The problem of pressure groups becomes almost inextricable from the general study of the political parties and the struggle for power (De Grazia, 2004). The political leader for the most part can be the individualist free to bargain and willing to deal with a variety of opposing groups for the sake of preservation of individual power and keeping the collective vision.

In certain situations, an individual can influence the political leader's perception of an equilibrium comfort level even if they do not belong to an organized group. Typically, these are persons with the potential to deliver influence or campaign funding that in the view of the political leader are important to keep loyal or neutral to the leader's agenda. These types of persons seek resolution for some issue that, if not addressed, can result in the withholding of influence and support, which in turn could lead to disequilibrium.

Through personal observation, I have seen that there are a limited number of individuals that yield such influence. It should be pointed out that the "politically active" public is relatively small compared to the total population. Even a not so politically connected or influential single citizen, inspired by an intense selfish or altruistic purpose, can exert an influence greatly disproportionate to his numerical influence as one of thousands of people.

From my own political activity and observation, I know that most experienced politicians can name a handfull of specific individuals in their constituencies who persist in making their influence felt.

Sources of disequilibrium

The sources of either process or system disequilibrium can arise from internal or external forces. The roots of either lie in the factors that set up the condition of tension. The typical internal sources are forces that choose to challenge the existing leadership. This type of challenge can be an assult on leadership process or it may also be an assult on the system in a way that brings into question the ability of the current political structure to achieve the mission and vision. Random external forces or organized opposition groups are the sources of system and process disequilibrium.

The source of motivation for external forces is an approach that is either anti-vision or anti-leader and will cause opposition to act in such a way as to attempt to disrupt the existing systems and processes to derail the leader and his vision. Interviews with community leaders and activists clearly note this planned disruption of the status quo was part of getting what they want by threatening the plans or mission of sitting political leaders. As one interviewee expressed, "I can be pretty hard-headed and a real pain in the ass until I am acknowledged."

Condition: Threat of Derailment

The threat of derailment is present when the political leader has detected that a state of tension and disequilibrium have reached a level of intensity that demands attention. The intensity level is such that to ignore the issues underlying the disequilibrium would result in political damage to the leader and divert focus and resources from the vision. This is clearly demonstrated with an observation of Kerry's presidential campaign. He is forced to pay attention to the attacks by independent Vietnam veteran groups that have attempted to discredit him. Clearly this need to respond and to reassure his support base has taken resources from promoting the vision and objective message.

Derailment threats tend to be of two types. These types are a threat to the political self, the personal attack on the individual or the attack on support coalitions with the sole purpose of fractioning the groups so that their strength is rendered ineffective in their ability to follow the vision and implement the mission.

The attacks on the individual political leader are direct threats that provide the possibility for a loss of power and or position through political defeat. The experienced political leader is keenly aware of the forces that have the ability to derail the political agenda and or the ability to limit or take political power.

An example of the threat of derailment occurred when community leadership was able to build support at the County Council level for a diversion of budget funds to support a number of requested actions for improving schools and increasing police presence. The potential transfer of funds from one set of programs to address the problems cropping up in Hilltop- threatened to slow or even eliminate a number of politically favorable programs of the county executive.

In addition, the reputation as effective political leader was now threatened which had a potential impact on several county re-election bids. The move to create political change through positive intervention can occur at any level of the social-political structure.

The first level as discussed here is the direct approach where the political leader reacts to political pressure. The objective here is the hope that the exerted influence is strong enough to threaten the powerbase of the political leader. The next level to attack is at the legislative level where attempts to either introduce or defeat proposed legislation takes place by mobilizing support and opposition groups. Next, political activists may be able to mute or lessen the impact of new legislation by seeking to attack at the bureaucratic program implementation level.

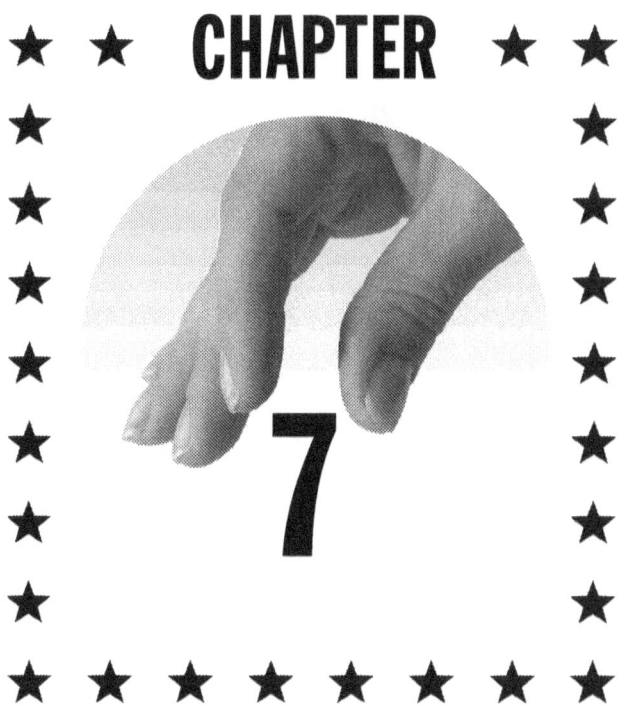

CHAPTER

7

How Politicians React
to Threats

Chapter 7

How Politicians React to Threats

Stage three of the political Shoring-up process is identified as the "reacting" stage where the threat of derailment is apparent and a reaction mode enables Shoring-up actions to protect the vision and the political leader. The component elements of this stage are "scanning", "assessing", and "diffusing". These activities are engaged in by political leaders to assess community attitudes and opinions in an effort to identify and address potential threats of derailment.

"Reacting" is the response to the conditions set in Sensing; stage one of Shoring-up. When a threat is discovered or implied, the process of knowing the opposition and the level and nature of their support is needed to mount any defensive action or offensive attack.

Scanning
Political survival and the ability to stay on the mission and vision are dependent upon an incumbent's ability to scan the political environment and determine areas of opportunity and areas of threat. According to a former county politician, "you had better know what's going on in your district or the opposition will use your lack of knowing like a club".

This stage begins with a political environmental scan. Scanning consists of monitoring of news media, community association publications, business associations and trade groups and as a former state senator expressed, just "being conscious of what is being said on the street". Additionally, scanning monitors and measures trends and elements of core community concerns such as crime rate, school performance, tax revenues, etc. When opportunities for increasing power and influence are seen from the scanning process, political leaders assess the strength of the resources they can bring to bear on taking advantage of the presented opportunity.

The external political environmental factors like those found in the business environment consist of several externalities that can pose either opportunity or threat to the political vision. Externalities by their nature are beyond the control of any group or individual. As such, the scanning process identifies changes in these externalities. The most common externalities that may impact public policy and political decisions are shifts or changes in; social, cultural, demographic, economic, and the legal and regulatory environments.

Socio-Cultural scans reveal subtle changes in or blending of sub-cultures in terms of values, norms, customs, language, or things related to religion and ethics. The data show that in the Hill Top and Lakeside case, several groups have contributed to some blending of sub-cultures, such as a young black community and an older, white community, which contributed to the creation of conflict that eventually led to the need for political intervention.

On a national level, I have witnessed the emergence of a significant Hispanic community, which caused government to respond by providing dual language requirements on all government forms in recognition of the growth in a Spanish-speaking constituency. In everyday life, Americans have seen cultural influences in the form of new food choices, the dominance of African-Americans on music and fashion. The experienced political leader is keenly aware of these influences and the need to identify new groups that can offer support or can be deemed a new threat to the mission. Social and cultural changes became evident in the case communities.

The influx of both Hispanic and Afro-American groups brought a change in each community's social and cultural fabric. A new diversity of thinking and points of view as to what community values should be held or honored added to the building tension within the community.

Demographic changes as seen in the case data for Hill Top and Lakeside offer another important set of variables for constant scanning. Issues related to aging and the geographic shifting of population offers the potential for dramatic changes in constituent needs and expectations that translate into changes in voting patterns. The patterns of age, income education and occupation have significant importance on the acquiring and disposition of resources. Demographic changes, not only in regard to race, were in play such as the aging and change of family life cycles for the established residents. Aging community residents, wanting to move onto either, retirement or other more suitable retirement lifestyles, found interaction with the newer entrants into the community difficult. Further, many home owners, in an effort to flee the situation, sold homes to investors who converted them to rental units and, therefore, changed the neighborhoods from owners to renters.

Within the seven-year period, the case communities became demographically reversed. The area now had considerably more renters than owner occupied properties, schools moved from the upper ten percent in state test scores to the lower ten percent matching nearby city.

Economic issues such as unemployment or lack of job growth and new business development and retention are major issues for the political leader. The leader that ignores changes or deficiencies in the economic environment is courting disaster. The presidency of George H. W. Bush was toppled by opposition that stressed that "It's the economy stupid". Political leaders are usually confronted with issues of income distribution and redistribution. Economic issues within the Hill Top community became the concern of the area merchants and service businesses.

The change in the demographic and socio-cultural mix had caused many to find their services and products not sought and in some cases not affordable. Many opted to abandon the area for more fruitful markets. Empty commercial property remained vacant for a long time. Retailers that catered to the new demographic took some, but not all, of the vacant space. Commercial property owners and remaining merchants attempted to exert political and economic pressure to cause some sort of protective action.

Legal, regulatory, and political environments are the battleground for political action. For every bit of legislation and regulatory enforcement, one group is protected or sheltered and the other group is the denied or restricted. The political Shoring-up process is most common, active, and open in this environment. Legal, regulatory, and political environment scans revealed a desire from competing groups for a variety of actions that political leaders were later forced to address. Some of the groups' demands were centered on methods to control the number of rental properties. Other issues focused on changing the criteria for evaluation and ranking of schools. Additionally, the pros and cons of increased police actions were the source of concern of minority groups.

Assessing, Pros, Cons and Political Cost

Information gathered during the scanning process is analyzed for the presence of current and potential future adversaries and the strengths and weaknesses of their positions. Assessing is a subjective evaluation by leadership of the strength of threats to the standing political vision and current agenda.

Assessing can also identify opportunities which can be enhanced by "Shoring-up" the support base of the vision. It is in this stage that political leadership assesses the environment as a political system. This systemic approach to assessment allows for the analysis of the consequences of actions or inaction. It is utilized to assess "what became imbalanced and why?" In addition, the effectiveness of any political intervention or acts of Shoring-up used to change or address problems within the political community are assessed. The political leader in effect looks at the external factors of the system namely the social, cultural, demographic elements, etc., to ascertain whether the type and level of imbalance, if any, are the result of status quo disruption.

The political leadership determined that the changes in the Hill Top-Lakeside communities were a political liability and demanded immediate attention and action.

Since these elements are out of the control of leaders, they must then take control of resources that can be controlled to address the environmental threat or opportunity and assess the interactions as a whole system. The failure to consider and understand the complex systems nature of a problem can result in problems of greater magnitude than the original problem of concern often because of unintended and unforeseen consequences (Simmons & Gregory, 2003). When all the elements of the system as developed by the political leader are in equilibrium, all actions work towards the fulfillment of the overall vision and mission. As an extension of the process, possible responses to a political threat are evaluated. Assessing process leads to an assessment of possible action or non-action. The political leader has three available options for Shoring-up action: offensive mode, holding mode and defensive mode.

Offensive mode

The use of an offensive mode strategy requires the politician to weigh the consequences of taking an attack posture. The assessment of the cost and benefits of such a strategy must be evaluated. The consequences of public opinion and the likelihood of a counter attack must be weighed. In the Hill Top community, some of the tension producing situations had a strong race component. A direct attack on the crime issue without some sensitivity to the racial underpinnings would have caused a swift and strong counter attack by the NAACP against the current political leadership.

Holding mode

Sometimes the assessment must include the option of doing nothing. In situations where all the forces and factors are as yet undetermined, this may be the logical approach according to a former county executive. "Sometime the willingness and the desire to act is not necessarily a virtue".

Some would argue that the swiftness of President Bush in invading Iraq was such a situation where staying in a holding mode may have been wiser. Others, of course, would point out that given the information he had, although inaccurate, the only choice was invasion.

Defending mode

The defending mode choice is basically sticking by your position and seeking to defend yourself, the vision and your supporters from an organized assault. If the assessment is to take on a defending mode, the strategies and tactics of justifying the position and seeking a rebalancing as soon as possible will be implemented.

Diffusing

The object of the diffusing strategy is first to lower or eliminate the tension, restore equilibrium and to reinstate the vision.

Elimination of the condition of disequilibrium requires that actions be taken to disburse or diffuse any opposition power. Diffusing is a process of convincing both loyal followers and opposition groups that a new equilibrium is in place. Accommodations are often made to opposition groups to lessen the threat. Loyal followers often feel that something was taken from their position in order to accommodate the opposition and to buy peace. Diffusing attempts to create a new equity equation where all sides buy into a new equity that delivers the parties to a new tentative equilibrium.

It is the object of this action to lower the tension. The action was designed to buy time and divert opposition groups from attacks on the sitting leadership and redirect their actions to some other activity such as some ad hoc committee. By using this tactic, the county executive was now in a power position and waited for the commission to offer solutions to which he could react.

The presence of new powerful alliances caused political leaders in the county to engage in Shoring-up behaviors through the creating of a community study commission with community leaders from all factions as members. This group was tasked with the mission of exploring new approaches for solving the problem. This move effectively moved the politicians from the immediate line of fire and kept their support groups in a lessened state of tension.

It is important to note that at no time was the issue of cause and effect relationships examined. The only output was a call for a search for actions that may stop or impede the emerging trends. This is what the political leader wants, because it removes him from the focus of the problem. Political leadership engaged in activity based on certain situational expectations of outcomes to obtain balance and preserve their power base (Vroom, 1995). The properties of diffusing are deflecting, leveling, and marginalizing.

Deflecting

Deflecting is a tactic designed solely as a method of buying time or dissipating the energy built up within opposition groups. It is used to give the impression to the community at large and the opposition groups that something is being done to address a community grievance. This tactic employs the use of having a "study" of the problem conducted. Other approaches include the naming of a "special" commission made up of mid-level officials and community leaders for the sole purpose of examining the issue and making recommendations to the official that employed the deflection tactic. Another ploy used to deflect and to buy time is to set up a series of prerequisites necessary to be solved before the main issue can become the focus of action. This misdirection, when successful, effectively derails opposition by blocking their effort to mount a counter offensive.

James Macgregor Burns (1978, p. 409) describes the process of political leaders as techniques of delay. He points out that particularly legislative decision-makers seek to defuse issues by setting up investigative or deliberating bodies that can report later when the public feeling has lost most of its intensity. The legislative and executive branches of government are not the only elements of government leadership to use this tactic. It is demonstrated in the judicial branch particularly by judges who face the election process versus appointment.

These judges seek technicalities to find a "hot" case moot or, if that fails, send the decision to a lower court for consideration. According to Burns, this is effective for postponing controversial constitutional questions until the public attitudes have "matured" or the tension of the issue eased. An incident from the county data clearly shows a situation where the Lakeside community lost a library due to budget cuts. The county executive was under intense pressure to re-open the facility. To deflect the community energy away from personal attacks on him; he challenged the community to find funds and volunteers to operate the facility and pledged support for a viable and solid plan.

The community to the surprise of the county executive came out in force. It was described best in an interview with the president of the community association.

"The power of the citizen -- we had used our little newsletter, the most effective weapon you have, putting out where people -- anybody that wants to get our library back, willing to serve on a committee, willing to do grassroots, distributing fliers or getting information out, or whatever, show up at this meeting on such-and-such a date. The Councilman rode over with the County Executive that night. The executive was telling the councilman, "they will not get this library; I can't afford to give them this library, they're not going to get this library. What's it going to be, 50 people there; they're just going to have to understand the economics. The County Executive walked into our very first organizing committee meeting of 350 people."

Although the end result was a surprise to the county executive, the deflection tactic did relieve the political pressure and even resulted in a solution that suited all sides and the image of the county executive was enhanced from the situation as a bonus political payoff.

Leveling

Leveling is a tactic of diffusing. This tactic utilizes any one or a combination of five actions in an effort to return to a state of equilibrium. This can take the form of compromising, a conceding a point, bargaining forward, empowering opposition and marginalizing.

Leveling actions are directed towards any faction that is judged to have influence and power to divert the vision or offer support for the leader and the vision. This means that leveling activity can be directed at both supporters who now feel aggrieved or political opponents who must be satisfied to the point of releasing the tension. Leveling gestures and perceptions are important components of the leveling process since they are designed to retain balance on all sides and not abandon the vision and mission of the majority.

Compromising

Analysis of data from my own political experience and simple observation of others involved in the political process demonstrates that compromising while still achieving your goals is the essence of politics. Finding common ground upon which to agree with the opposition allows a level of Incrementalism and gives all sides of a debate enough satisfaction to discourage continued opposition. This action has as its' sole purpose the protection of the vision from derailment.

Conceding

The concession or favor to political supporters is offered as a means of assuring the "faithful" that they have not been abandoned in favor of competing opposition groups. It is, in fact, an admission of momentarily diverting from the mission and vision in favor of dealing with an opposition demand. The offered concession, or favor is not a major action that is likely to re-energize the opposition.

In my own experience when faced with the need to engage leveling, I found myself offering recommendations for positions of prestige on boards or committees that had little power. In other circumstances, I was able to offer seats of honor at highly visible public functions with state and national dignitaries. In dealing with the opposition, the process is similar with the major distinction being that the purpose is to encourage peace. Typical actions would include a public statement on how valuable their insight and suggestions were in obtaining a solution.

Observation of the interchange between President George W. Bush and Senator Edward M. Kennedy reveal such a leveling action. Kennedy was allowed to author the "No child left behind" legislation. The President gave him public praise and was given full credit for his work. This quieted the education critics and took an issue away from the opposition. Bush, however, was less than happy with all of the provision of the bill, which he signed into law.

As a result, he structured other legislation that hampered the funding of the new laws provisions that he opposed. Bush had conceded the point that a National education bill was needed to appease the Democrats. On the other hand, the President appeased his supporters by blocking funding. In this case the President could boast that he supported both sides.

Bargaining Forward

This is an interesting tool used by politicians in leveling. It is basically an agreement to offer assistance or an offer not to oppose some future action in exchange for current support. The NAACP was seeking to intervene in the Hill Top situation. In exchange for a muted stance against the county executive's position on increased policing of troubled areas, the county executive offered future support the following year in creating a new predominant Black council district that would insure a Black seat on the current all white male council.

The bargaining forward promise was accepted by the NAACP and kept by the executive the following year.

Empowering Opposition

Empowering opposition is a leveling tool that gives the opposition the opportunity to structure the solution. This process in the county situation resulted in the community passing on the opportunity, but the county executive had gained the upper hand and deflected future problems in the development of the community, because the buck was passed back to him.

As the then Director of Community Development put it: "We didn't come up with a detailed plan. What we wanted to do was form a committee of all -- with all the interested community associations having membership on this committee to explore and develop what would be appropriate...for that site. Now the one thing we had decided would be it would be a housing site. And what happened was, some people were critical of us because we didn't have a detailed plan to show them; and I told them we didn't have a detailed plan because we wanted them to be a part of the plan."

This attempt at empowering opposition worked better than planned. When offered the task of coming up with a plan they found it much easier to criticize than come up with a solution. The area politicians could not believe their good fortune in that the opposition provided the instrument of their own defeat. I have seen other examples where the opposition was allowed to give solutions within the pre-arranged parameters and guidelines and did so. This allowed for a diffusion of the imbalance tension through an empowering leveling strategy.

Marginalizing

The ability to marginalize opponents is an absolute necessity for the political leader. Being skillful in this tactic can diffuse the most difficult instances of disequilibrium. The process of marginalization is to take potentially powerful opposition and find way to make them a non-factor without the targeted opposition leader realizing what has happened until after the tension has subsided and a form of equilibrium has returned.

The data from the case studies of Hill Top indicate several instances where marginalizing occurred. The first example was that of elected officials setting up the citizen's commission to study the causes of problems in the community. Fearing racial backlash for increased policing of Hill Top, the

most visible and vocal Black leaders were invited to participate only to have themselves not as members presenting final
recommendation to the county executive. That was left to
the existing elected community association members. This
pushing to the side accomplished several things that assisted
the success of Shoring-up. First, tensions were immediately
decreased with the formation of the commission.

Second, a tentative equilibrium was established, which
allowed the political leadership to focus on their agenda and
vision. Third, and most importantly, the opposition was
"sucked" into the process and rendered powerless through
being marginalized.

CHAPTER

8

Politicos love to Kick Ass!
- Then Make Nice

Chapter 8

Politicos love to Kick Ass! - Then Make Nice

After engaging in a political confrontation, the political victor needs to return the political environment to a stage of equilibrium as soon as possible. Politicians pride themselves in this ability to normalize the situation to the new equilibrium, which could leave the opposition no better off then when the process began. For the community leader who came up short in the confrontation; a decision to accept defeat or continue the battle must happen at this stage. Allowing a new equilibrium will in most cases marginalize your efforts and your leadership.

I have labeled this stage of behavior as "normalizing". This behavior is designed to bring the political environment back into the new status quo and returns the political focus toward reaching the mission and goals that support the vision.

Normalizing consists of three actions: justifying, reinforcing, and consolidating. Political leaders engage in this stage of Shoring-up when threats and adversaries have been neutralized. The situation however still needs to be eliminated from the public focus. The justifying action is directed at two groups: the support group and the opposition.

Supporter Justifying

Justifying is the tactic engaged to mollify the support base if a leader's actions are open to a negative interpretation by their support base. Methods of justifying are centered on three concepts that are the root of all public policy. These are *fairness, harmony, protecting the vision.*

The political leader uses these concepts to create a reasonable basis for actions taken, therefore, justifying her/his actions.

A politician's appeal for *fairness* in justifying their actions refers to the principle of treating "likes alike".

Political leaders that face criticism for their action may appeal to the political base's sense of fairness.

Harmony is the attempt to get to a state of acceptance and agreement in order to move on to other issues. It is the validation of the approaches or actions. In terms of justifying, the extent of harmony is a measure of the level of disruption to vision. The measure of the harmony of any political action is based on two questions: Has the mission or vision been co-opted for the long run? Does the action have the potential to disrupt power and control? If the answers to these questions is "no", then the leader's behavior can be legitimately "justified" to the majority constituency as the most efficient way of addressing the issue without threatening the vision.

The leader uses the concept of *protecting the vision* to justify that the actions taken, while objectionable to some, were done to protect the ideals and values of the group and protect the mission.

Opposition Justifying

Justifying methods are directed towards the opposition in order to mollify the desire to continue the creation of tension and disequilibrium. The data suggest that the presence of two elements is important in returning to a political balance. The first is the importance to acknowledge the opposition's position. That does not mean the agreement or acceptance of the position.

If possible, the political leader attempts to explain why it was impossible at the present time to give the opposition all that they wanted. In the Hill Top case, the county executive was able to mollify minority groups by pointing out that he had created opportunities for home ownership, which would eventually improve the area. That action would, in turn, create the need for less police patrols when the community stabilized. This would, in the long run, be what the minority groups had sought.

At the same time, supporters received the support of more police on the streets until the negative environment could be reduced. The minority opposition groups could see that they got something significant in that the leader is now sensitive to their views. It is important that the leader not give the impression that the demands of the opposition were unreasonable.

This acceptance of the opposition position is for the sole purpose of keeping lines of communication open. In the political process, it is inevitable that the leader will have future need of the opposition's support and political leaders are very cognizant that today's political opponent is tomorrow's ally.

The second element that the political leader must invoke during the justifying process is what is referred to in political campaigns as the "fifty percent plus one rule". This is a reminder to the opposition as to who is in the political majority.

The current political leadership points out that though leaders are cognizant of the oppositions position and desires, the fact remains that at the moment at least fifty percent of the voters, plus one additional person, supports the current vision and mission. This is a necessary affirmation of political power.

Reinforcing the Base

The purpose or reinforcing is simply to solidify the base.

The process uses techniques that motivate. This is usually accomplished with the method of reward and punishment. In reinforcing change, the process of unfreezing is an alteration of the forces acting on an individual such that his stable equilibrium is disturbed sufficiently to motivate him to make him ready for change. Changing is the actual process of learning a new attitude or behavior. Refreezing is integration of the new attitude into the new personality.

In the case of reinforcing, the unfreezing action is caused by the outside disturbance, which caused a disruption of the equilibrium. Instead of seeking a changing behavior, the political leader uses his influence and power in taking actions that solidify loyalty to the leader through the use of rewards and the threat of punishment and refreezes a new balanced equilibrium that supports the vision. This, in essence, refreezes the new equilibrium processes and behaviors that still support the original vision.

In addition, it is a time when the leader will attempt to bring former opponents to whom concessions were made back into the follower base. This leads to the strategy of mobilizing to expand the base of followers thus moving to a process of consolidating supporters and members of the former opposition group.

Consolidating Regained Power

For the political leader, consolidating has one main goal; that is the gathering and control of the collective power and establishing a re-balancing of the political environment. Consolidating is a two-pronged process.

The first prong is to bring the collective power of diverse support groups and individuals under the influence and control of the political leader. The second prong of consolidating deals with the relationship with opposing, but now defeated factions. This requires a process of building a limited consensus among opposition members and groups to support a higher order of principles such as patriotism, goodwill, or survival of the community as a community. This approach is one in which conflict is muted for the short-term through the political leaders acknowledgement that "we can all agree to disagree" on a point but, in the long run, the community regards itself as a singular entity, striving for a higher principle of unity.

The political leader ultimately understands that consolidating is at best a process that leads to a temporary condition or state that may be viewed by those outside the community as a consensus. As Burns points out, "Political culture does change, and the mechanics and dynamics of this change set the stage for later leadership emergence and conflict. Few societies are immune in the long run to fundamental economic and social changes that bring in their wake forces of social...and political change" (Burns, 1978, p. 84).

In a case where political actions are needed to insure the short-term gains of Shoring-up, behaviors routinely consist of attempts to overpower any opposition to the interventions instituted to bring equilibrium. The decisions that confront the leadership involved two basic questions: Can political action insure the stability of the community? Secondly, can political action aid in creating a positive perception of a detrimental situation? These issues are most certainly constrained by situational variables and the political and community leadership's abilities to deal with the interpersonal dynamics required in reaching the desired results of equilibrium.

That result is an acceptable negotiated level of community wellness, which is a critical element in the goal of consolidating power. On the local political level it was a matter of using shoe leather and pressing the flesh. As one former county executive put it: "We'd go out to a community and would try to identify the pro and con administration community activists...people that were actively involved in their community in one form or another, bring them all together into a planning process".

This exercise of political influence is what Burns (1978, p. 434) refers to as the "authoritative allocation of values" that are considered the legitimate use of power. Political power is linked in the moment by legitimacy tied to a constitution with the authority to form a government. However, the exercising of this power is not without consequences from constituents and other legislative and political foes.

In consolidating, political leaders pull together the power of the varied constituencies to establish a united front against opposition groups. It should be noted that consolidating is an exercise, not of compromise, but a display of political power without providing the fuel for continued confrontation. That power has been effectively used to quiet or defeat opposition to the political leader's mission and agenda.

It is a demonstration of political victory and putting on notice for any potential future opposition, the level of power held by the leader. For those who live the political life, victory over opposition is the ultimate high.

CHAPTER

9

Political Power as a zero Sum Game

Chapter 9

Political Power as a zero Sum Game

The political benefits of Shoring-Up

In our current political system, politicians do not have the luxury of actually solving social problems. The short life cycles of elected office in most cases makes it difficult to attack the causes for negative social phenomenon. Our collective demand for instant remedy doesn't allow government officials the time or resources to attack the causes of social discontent. This limits some type of permanent solution of complex social issues.

Indeed the cost in political capital in the form of a public's demand for retribution for failed attempts may put the price of trying to solve problems out of the reach of most politicians. While similar to the management process of "Satisficing" introduced by Herbert A. Simon in **Models of Man** (1957), a process where the objective is to find a solution, the process of Shoring-Up is not the same. "Satisficing" seeks to solve the problem with the first usable solution that is not necessarily the best solution. Satisficing is an alternative to optimization for cases where there are multiple and competitive choices in which one gives up the idea of obtaining a "best" solution.

In contrast, the process of Shoring-Up means addressing the problem in such a way as to relieve political pressure without any attempt at a final or temporary solution of the real problem. Because political decisions are not necessarily oriented to solve the real problem but to relieve political pressure, any directed attempt at a short-term solution is not sustainable as a permanent solution over the long haul. The winds of political fortune or discontent will ultimately force another decision on the same issues.

The Shoring-Up process model can be considered the direct response to a lack of trust in the public's ability to accept hard decisions that have the potential for asking for sacrifice on the part of any group. The public has in recent history demonstrated resistance to good decisions versus good political solutions.

In such a case, the public interests want solutions that are satisfactory to the political powerbase and not the society as a whole. This requires the political office holder to pander to the desires of groups or coalitions of groups that can pressure for the desired results. How else can we legitimately explain the political necessity for sidestepping issues such as; the long term viability of the U.S. Social Security System. In this case, political leaders seem to willing to bet that they will all be out of office and dead when the crap hits the fan.

Political ideology drives the direction of Shoring Up. Non-partisanship is neither possible nor is it desirable for those that implement Shoring Up strategies. The process of Shoring-Up is a partisan activity. It requires the pitting of one group's interest against another. In political terms, for the survival of the politician and their vision and mission, it is necessary for one set of principles to win and opposition to be vanquished.

The political activist knows and average citizens must come to realize that no matter how just, or noble, a cause may be, unless the perpetuators of that cause can gain political clout, then the cause is likely to die on the vine.

The necessity of this political behavior can be exhibited in the earliest of human interactions. In what has been referred to as the "Model of Triads", a basic observable action occurs in any schoolyard or in pre-school sandbox. The simple viewing of three children at play will eventually demonstrate Shoring-Up activity. When all three are in agreement they tend to "play nice" or, what I would refer to in the political sense, be in "equilibrium".

Within Figure 1.0 below, we can observe an even give and take between all participants. There is a balance in the relationships in that each participant is free to give and accept interaction between the parties. This phenomenon is equally true whether we are expressing behavior between individuals within a group or between independents.

Inevitably, with the passage of time this equilibrium will become threatened when one entity seeks some advantage, favor or demands from or preference over another party even at the expense of the other. At this point in time, members

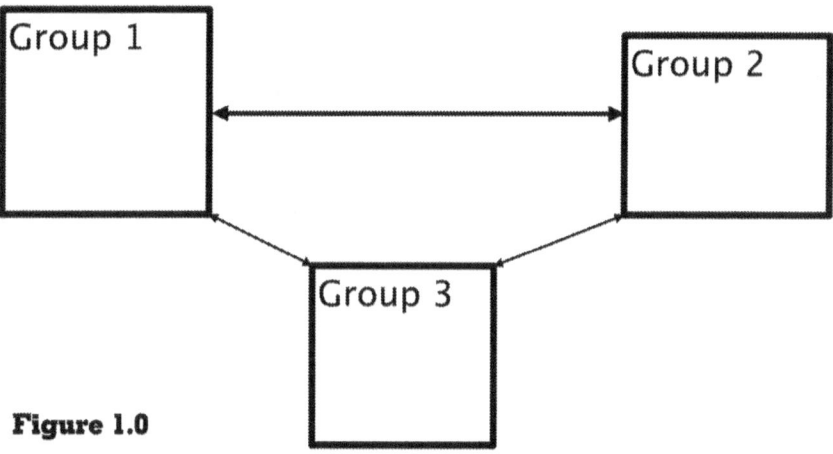

Figure 1.0

of the group choose to either side with the "active" player or reject the demands and seek to deny the actions of the seeker of the favor. If the rejected member complies then equilibrium is re-established. However if the rejected member seeks control, he often will attempt to form an alliance against the actions of the rejecting party. This, in effect, creates a new dynamic and grouping which acts to deny membership to the former "power holder".

Figure 2.0 below, illustrates the forming of an alliance against the "out" or "offending" entity. Entity one and Entity two have formed an alliance with each other to form a barrier of exclusion to Entity "3".

The now 'Ousted' entity will now be forced into one of three choices: First, leave the group and seek another group to which membership is extended. This is indicated by the broken arrow of entity one; Second, the entity could try persuading one of the members of the alliance to break ranks and form a new alliance or; Third, as seen most commonly within the context of political behavior, the expelled member, if they have limited or no access to power, influence or incentives, will make concessions, promises or take action that will re-establish the harmony in an attempt to return the system to equilibrium.

Shoring-Up's Situational Environment

This example is the basic political struggle of maintaining harmony among cultural communities in order to fortify and hold together the political community. The most highly con-

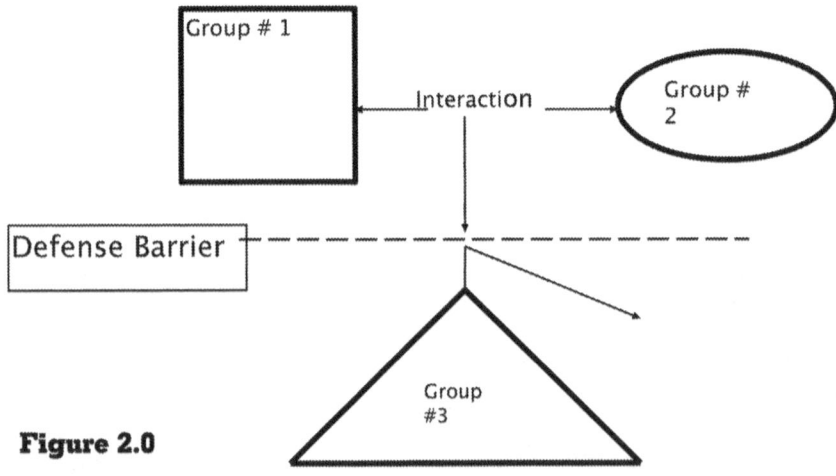

Figure 2.0

tested and passionate political fights are about membership or exclusion (Stone, 2002, p19.). The politics of inclusion or exclusion is the basis for all political activity. The ability of political leaders to maintain a state of equilibrium is central to their ability to hold power and influence. This requires engaging in that old playground phenomenon of "Shoring-Up the relationships that not only keep you in the group but keeps the political leader in power.

The need for Shoring-Up activity stems from the basic requirement that leaders must constantly strive to keep followers focused on a mutual mission, eliminate or neutralize dissent and maintain the state of equilibrium. It is the strength of the mission and the leader's ability to articulate that mission is the glue that holds the political community together.

The beginnings of Change

It is vitally important to the citizen and the political activist to understand this process in order to affect change for the benefit of the constituency groups and to put these changers of the political environment on equal footing with the professional manipulators of public policy- the elected political leader.

Probably the best way to understand and to recognize the process of Shoring-up is in the examples that were used in the Hilltop and Lakeside case studies. My personal experience, as a community development consultant, tells me that this same process is played over and over in most American communities.

Anywhere democratic societies function, elected and appointed political leaders find the issues surrounding the maintenance of community wellness a continuous challenge.

An excellent place to begin the explanation of how Shoring-up is utilized by political operatives is simply to observe them in action. The social and political problems that arise as the by products of the attempts to maintain political communities in a proper balance offers the greatest opportunity to observe and experience how political leaders struggle to balance factors. If left un-checked, these factors would cause a threat to the political leaders power and office. When this imbalance becomes noticeable, it is common for these leaders to seek actions that address the symptoms of the distress in an effort to avert or lessen a building tension. More often than not, this action requirement must be made in context of the political necessity for sidestepping issues such as; the long term viability of the U.S. Social Security System.

Disruptions and therefore shocks to the quality of life within the system require changes that call for the political intervention. Political leaders responding to these changes often react by using Shoring up activity to address the perceived changes on the community system leading to disequilibrium.

Why Real Problems Must Go Unsolved

Some problems go unsolved simply because they are too difficult or too politically charged for any political leader to take on without political fallout. Often, those with the political will to address real social problems tend to fall short because politicians are forced by constituents to address the negative symptoms on an immediate basis. This pressure requires a "band Aid" approach.

As stated in a previous chapter, citizens force this approach because we are reluctant or perhaps just unwilling to pay the price for the elimination of the true causes of social and or economic problems. Part of this behavioral phenomenon is the recognition by citizens and politicians alike that we are dealing with complex entrenched social systems. As such, any real cure would require the dismantling and a total redesign of the entire system, not the piecemeal approach that is usually engaged to attack the system. The usual approach as described in the earlier case example creates what we all recognize as the "unintended consequences" of the politically correct actions.

To be fair, political and public service life is a difficult job. The process of community development and preservation are continuous challenges for both local governments and community leaders. Often the problems of community decline are met with politically expedient short term interventions that are aimed at specific system components for the purpose of addressing symptoms and maintaining political equilibrium. This has been done in some cases without an understanding of the cause and effect relationships that lead to the visible symptoms in the first place.

The Political Decision Making System in Operation

In order to influence a political decision or action, those who wish to exert influence needs to establish an environment of disequilibrium. Politicians do not respond to "Normal." They only respond to things that take them outside of their comfort zone.

Not only does the decision process need to be interrupted, the decision making systems that surround the political process needs to be attacked to the point that the system can not continue until the problem presented is addressed.

The decision making process within government happens on three levels. The first is the elected political office holder. The second level is made of those political influential that gain appointment to executive levels of the bureaucracy. The third level is the career civil servant class, who is theoretically apolitical and is protected from political power through the merit system.

We have examined the political behavior of elected officials and the Shoring-up behaviors in which they engage to protect their political capital and powerbase. Additionally, we can see the same behaviors in the political appointee level. These officials have a vested interest in the political safety of the groups that appointed them to office. Just as the elected class, this appointed group moves to protect their position through their protection of the politician responsible for their power position.

If your attack is now focused on the bureaucratic and administrative levels of government, being a known entity will more than likely allow you access to the three levels mentioned above. Once allowed access, you have in fact been acknowledged as someone with power.

A Citizen's strategy for Change
The attempt to influence political or public policy can be directed at anyone of the three levels. The threat to political power is the primary approach. Attacking existing policy can be directed at the legislative level by mobilizing opposition groups to create an on mass show of force. The second and third levels are a continuance of a battle that may have been previously thwarted at the elected official level.

The ability of political activists to stop, implement or impede legislation or executive orders can be realized at executive appointed levels of the bureaucracy and the career civil servant class.

Activists with the appropriate amounts of real or perceived clout can cause a political appointee and the career bureaucrat to limit or impede legislative action. Most citizens do not know that legislative bodies frequently pass a bill that has broad popular appeal only to scrap or defeat the enabling legislation for that same bill by not funding the program or authorizing the acquisition of personnel to carryout the legislative mandate. This process allows cover for those who appose an action but don't want it to be public knowledge. The results are classic Shoring-up. Politicians take credit for addressing an issue only to do the opposite when it comes to funding a program.

More often than not, the implementation of a political decision falls to the government bureaucracy that administers the political decision of elected officials. It is possible to have this bureaucracy interpret and implement programs in a way that is inconsistent to the original intent of the political forces initiating the action.

It is this fact that can give the community activist and individuals seeking to influence change another opportunity to have impact even after losing the battle in the elected official arena.

If we examine the world of the political bureaucracy, it, just as the political leader, is influenced by any outside effort that has the potential to create an environment of instability.

The decision making systems of government are in constant motion-colliding-overlapping and often competing for limited resources. In order to influence this system, the would-be activist needs to watch closely and acquire the skills needed to maneuver the bureaucratic leadership in the desired direction.

Such maneuvering is time consuming, intricate and in many ways highly specialized. It is precisely this process that political leaders and their appointed counterparts depend upon to wear you down.

It is this process that has spawned the emergence of so many lobbying organizations that are used because the effective participation in government decision making has become a full time job for some special interest groups.

As you have probably assessed, this is a daunting task. It is no wonder that the average citizen gives up or doesn't even bother. That is how the system is designed. This is precisely why citizens need to create a little disequilibrium.

How to Work the System
To gain the political upper hand you need facts. The more you know the more effective you will be in moving the opposi-

tion. Information becomes your fuel. The reality is you can't do this alone but you don't necessarily need an army. Some of the best sources and allies are the specialized press.

Specialty presses put out everything from newsletters, to slick monthly publication magazines for those in the industry. These usually have a vested interest since these sources are likely to be the public information arm for the specialized associations and trade groups. There are hundreds perhaps even thousands now with the internet as a source.

The ability of political activist to stop, implement or impede legislation can be realized at this level even if previous efforts are rebuffed at the elected official level. Activist, with the appropriate amounts of real or perceived clout can cause a political appointee to limit or impede legislative action. Likewise, congress and other legislative bodies frequently pass a bill that has broad popular appeal only to scrap or defeat the enabling legislation for that same bill by not funding the program or authorizing the acquisition of personnel to carryout the legislative mandate. The results are classic Shoring-up. Politicians take credit for addressing an issue only to do the opposite when it comes to funding a program.

Activist can effectively kill political decisions by understanding the elements within the system that are responsible for implementation of any policy and its related programs. Lee Fritschler and Bernard Ross in their book "How Washington Works" offers the following five steps;

1. Define the issue as precisely as possible. Be able to explain fully just what aspect of the new policy is the center for concern.
2. Locate the codified code (Law) that was created by the legislation.
3. Identify the agency assigned responsibility for implementation and oversight of the new policy. Additionally I rec-

ommend that you identify the legislative sub-committees responsible for funding.

4. Identify the groups such as, corporations, trade associations, unions, non-profit groups and other individuals interested in the policy. This includes pro and con groups.
5. Find the names of program participants and beneficiaries. Know their positions and why they take them.

The County, State and Federal code is a compendium of legislation passed by the legislators within these jurisdictions. It can be used to identify the answers to the above tasks. Additionally at the Federal level the *U.S. Government Manual*, is the most comprehensive source to agencies, bureaus and offices of government including the Executive branch.

Once the appropriate agency is located, the person to locate is the public information officer. This contact can help identify the progress of the new policy and all the special features including budget allocations and other important regulations attached to the implementation of the new policy or law.

To observe and appreciate the process within the bureaucratic decision making system in action you also need to understand the environment in which this decision making process takes place. While legislation, and in some cases the Constitution, may have established the agency; there is nothing in most legislation and certainly not in the U.S. Constitution any prescription for the management of the bureaucracy. In fact the structure of the management team in a divided or shared power environment makes it difficult for government officials to manage programs. This situation has often sparked debate between those favoring central versus those promoting decentralized control and power, on how much power and oversight politicians should have over these policy implementation agencies. As such the decision making systems have evolved to some sort of middle ground by informally bridging the separate powers. It is through this bridged system that all factors of government come together to make compromise on how implementation will be done, develop "real" public policy, and manage mandated programs. It is at this point that even defeated community action groups can thwart or lessen the impact of adverse political actions (Fritschler and Ross).

Just as the politician seeks to avoid disequilibrium in his environment, the constitutionally created bureaucracy seeks to stabilize the uncertainty and flux that is under constant pressures. When the actions of citizens can de-stabilize the situation public managers seek accommodation. These systems and agencies are basically held together by government officials who fear the consequences of a de-stabilized policy that threatens their very jobs. Citizen activist can and do benefit from the chaos of de-stabilization through delays and program modifications. The mere threat of actions to de-stabilize can cause effective compromise. Politicians also place a high premium on keeping the bureaucratic decision making system together because without it any kind of program implantation is impossible. Consequently, there is substantial incentive from all parties to compromise.

Attempts at attacking the system processes

If community activists are confronted with a bureaucracy that has closed out new participants by effectively denying access and accountability, they might find it easier to change the system. Believe it or not, it is easier than you might think. While the political systems seek equilibrium and stability; it also has created methods to change.

There are essentially two methods to accomplish change. The first approach is as suggested throughout this book, is to work through the system. That means supporting the system while using it to force change. In fact I recommend using the opposition's use of power within the system much like the Judo wrestler uses his opponent's power in charging against him. In short make the actions of an opponent work against him. This means seeking incremental change through the logical and legal manipulation of the people, methods, and system structure. This is done through attempts at persuasion to modify positions. The activist may even find that an offer to work for the re-election and support of current official will yield positive results. Offering ways to support your opposition's goals while still reaching your goals is the ultimate Display of political acumen. Using your opposition's own power to get what you want is what I have referred to as Judo Politics.

When this approach fails to achieve modification of public policy, the alternative approach is to bring about a new decision making system via a change in the political structure. If the old or current system is eliminated or blocked in the decision process, or if forced to allow other agencies to share in the decisions made, then the results are likely to be different. Astute community activists have been successful in having other agencies of government take up their cause by having them act on aspects of the proposed policy change that may have some minor impact on the other agency and its political constituencies. By simply encouraging the alternative agency to exert some authority on the policy, it is likely to dilute or lessen the original impact. In some instances the implication of the other agency could totally defeat the impact of the new legislation.

Other approaches available are that of redefining the issue. This is difficult and more often than not leads to a defeat and is a method of last resort. All public issues can be defined in two or more different perspectives. Moving the publics concept of position on the topic can sometime yield dramatic results. Having the politician's supports constituency see the topic from other perspectives that illuminate the unintended consequences of their previous position on the issue can help erode the original support from the political powerbase. Obviously such a shift would cause a new disequilibrium causing the political process to react. This disequilibrium also creates the opportunity to link others with the same view and therefore establish new coalitions. In this circumstance, old adversaries now are likely to work together to undo the previous legislation or policy.

Another approach is to escalate the issue to higher levels of the decision making system. On the Federal level this might be bringing the issue to the Cabinet or the President establishing a potential for political disequilibrium. On the state or local level, we seek to bring in the governor and or the top level state secretaries or on the county level-department heads. While typically decision making for program implementation does not occur at this level, the power of these positions to exert influence is enough to modify operational levels and program implementation.

Strengths and Weaknesses of the System (how to attack it)

Political and public policy decisions are typically a mix of ideology and pragmatism that are characteristic of American political life. The U.S. Constitution works at preserving the basis for the collective ideology at any point in time and the purposeful act of fragmenting and dispersing power throughout the system. In fact the system, even if we are postulating some failures, works remarkably well in balancing conflicting goals of a democracy which tend to be a balance between balancing power and management efficiency.

Bargaining and Incrementalism

Fritschler & Ross point out that a programmed focused decision systems are by necessity is pluralistic, depend upon bargaining strategies and efficiencies of the involved parties, and move incrementally. This process tends to support the status quo to a certain extent but the truth is that radical change is rare in government institutions. Change comes slowly if we are trying to do it at the bureaucratic level. But if we lost our attempt at change through the legislative process, or through the earlier attempts at political intimidation, then the bureaucracy becomes the vehicle of choice because most political and legislative decision systems allow for outside access from a variety of social economic and ethnic groups for the sole purpose of advancing their own interest. These groups in order to be successful in advancing an agenda must learn to bargain with each other over their conflicting interest through the use of their legislative and bureaucratic allies. This process is the same whether a special interest groups is seeking some advantage or attempting to block or limit the agenda of a competing group.

It is possible to have the bureaucratic structure offering contradictory programs which have the effects of negating an activist targeted program. An obvious example of government support for opposing programs can be seen in anti-smoking programs while at the same time government provides agricultural support programs for tobacco. In this case both sides have legitimate interests that are supported through government contradiction. The key here was to get a coalition to promote economic issues for the farmers without a directed attack against the anti-smoking crowd which was a health issue. It was relatively easy for both the politician and the bureaucracy to support health and positive economic supports.

Some might legitimately question the ability of activist to influence fundamental or major changes at the agency or bureau level. Many existing programs are well entrenched and seem to become immortal but this should not stop activist from trying to make change at this level if that is your target. The most promising area however as we indicated earlier is for new programs following new legislation. It is here that opponents of new legislation can have dramatic impact in the implementation.

CHAPTER

10

How to Counteract
Shoring-up Behaviors

Chapter 10

How to Counteract Shoring-up Behaviors

As stated earlier, the four stages of "shoring-up" are forging, sensing, reacting, and normalizing. Although there are a variety of steps in each stage, and a variety of situations and strategies in each step; a relatively few approaches will prove to be adequate defense to "Shoring-up" behaviors. The important thing to be remembered about the shoring-up process is that any stage, or any step, or any strategy is used as needed. Those using the process do not necessarily follow a prescribed order of events but simply enter the process at any point depending on current circumstances.

In other words, everything possible will be done to secure political power. The only criterion is what works. The only judgment whether something works is whether or not it helps strengthen or secure one's political power.

Use Shoring-up to advantage
Whereas it is impossible to design a behavioral intervention strategy that would cause all politicians to change their mode of operation, it is possible to develop defenses and counter attacks to limit the power of Shoring-up as a political offensive tool.

The political process is a contest, and as a contest, there are opportunities for both politicians and constituents to win in a given political struggle or event.

A suggested partial strategic option which is based on the shoring-up behavioral model is illustrated below. Politicians effectively secure and protect their power by knowing exactly "**when**" and "**how**" to adopt certain strategies to achieve specific goals that will lead to protecting one's power.

Constituents or political opposition can maximize their leverage with politicians by understanding **when, how** and **why** politicians behave in certain ways and how to use that understanding to negotiate with politicians to advance their own best interest. At the same time, opposition groups need to find viable ways in assisting politicians in securing their goals.

The issue in influencing politicians is in the power-centeredness of all politicians. This problem is obviously rampant and non-solvable. It makes them seek political office and to fight to hold on to it. However, some actions might be taken on the part of opposition groups, to make politicians react in ways that create some good in the process of securing their own power. Such opposition actions will be based on allowing the politician to support their own interest in securing power. However, they need their constituents to secure that power. This is why and how constituents can negotiate with politicians. Activists in order to advance their interests must help politicians secure their interests.

Possible Defensive Actions

The political process needs partisan constituencies to have a "shoring-up" political process. It is the action of both politicians as well as the opposition that makes up what we refer to as politics. Therefore, both politicians and their opponents can take some actions in each of the four stages of "shoring-up" that seeks to gain political advantage. A few illustrative actions in each stage are listed below:

Forging Stage:

This is the earliest stage at which a fledgling politician is beginning to establish a following and his powerbase. At this stage an aspiring politico is more likely to be open to some compromise instead of battling potential opposition. If the candidate for office believes that you have the willingness and the ability to block their path to power, they will adjust their approach.

The activists should form opposition groups with common ideological beliefs which can imply power and therefore have some influence over the targeted politicians.

Potential opposition groups can sometimes gain favor if they are able to clearly identify and articulate to the politician what benefits can be gained, such as; what can be offered of value to enhance a political position. This at some time has to become the expression of support for the politician in exchange of benefits from politicians. This whole process is contingent upon the ability of opposition groups to find support sufficient enough to provide at least the illusion of power.

Sensing Stage

In many ways it sometimes plays to your advantage not to flex too much muscle, particularly if you really have it. You can use it later.

Too bold of an approach sometimes forces the politician into a responsive fight mode. Activist groups can sometimes win points by being sensitive to the politician's natural instincts for self preservation. If the political opponent is in full "sensing" mode, then the use of overt threats and claims of existing or potential coalitions may be best unspoken. In the face of these threats the tendency is to defend ones political position.

Given these precautions, activist groups must be clear with what the groups wants. Activists must stay with group core values and principles to avoid loss of credibility through a willingness to unduly compromise these principles for a less than optimum resolution. A loss of credibility simply provides your opponent with the wedge issue he needs to power leverage your attack into a fully marginalized cause.

Reacting Stage

If you are seeking to challenge a sitting political leader, be mindful of an incumbent's ability to apply retribution. The activist must be aware of the current environment. It may produce situations where being responsive and flexible to politician's needs may yield benefits.

Always be ready to find common ground without giving too much in order to reach your goals. Politicians would rather be in a position of not having to react to outside pressure groups. Reacting to outside pressure is done only as a matter of shoring up their position and support.

Political opposition groups would be wise to not create a confrontation in the beginning phases of trying to get one's way. It is political instinct that will drive the sitting political power to seek the elimination of confrontational forces. Instead the strategy should be seeking methods that will eliminate the reasons to react in a negative manner. In other words, can a way be found to promote the needs of the politicians and at the same time meet the goals of the citizens group?

Normalizing Stage

In this stage, a victorious politician credits and rewards supporters of politicians/constituents, welcome the converted, forgive the die-hard and extend an invitation to come together. For the defeated activist, know that other avenues are open to reach your goals. It also is good political sense to drop the combative or competitive stance. Professional politicos know that is the way the "game rules" are. It is important that opposition groups can demonstrate their knowledge of the game. This has dividends in future battles.

The Shoring-Up model offers the activist tools and strategies based upon a rich explanatory behavioral process. The model identifies and prescribes behaviors and reactions exhibited by political leaders. My experience as a political candidate and as a political appointee has led me to believe that elected political leaders do want to effect positive change within their communities and the nation. However; the nature of political office is one in which political leaders are constantly facing the threat of derailment brought on primarily by constituent's constant demand for immediate solutions which in turn forces Shoring-Up activity.

As has been demonstrated, Shoring-Up actions divert efforts away from actions that could seek a final solution to many of the issues that American and global democracies face. Given that Shoring-Up, at the very least, delays final solutions, it is imperative that community leaders seek an approach to political intervention that promotes or encourages real solutions to community issues and problems. Certainly it is to the benefit of all parties to find effective and final solutions.

Shoring-Up tends to be reactionary and defensive.
Community leaders need to find methods and approaches that will allow political leaders to seek long term social solutions. The process needs to be a positive and proactive action from the point of view of the political leader to insure that the political vision is not threatened. Without the threat of derailment; the state of disequilibrium can not be put into play. It would be useful to community leaders to find ways to envelop the solutions to community problems into the achievement of the political vision.

The first step for the community leader is discovering what approach gets things done. In this context, the problem becomes how can community leaders short circuit the Shoring-Up behaviors that lead to non-solution actions by political leaders and more importantly what process will encourage actions that seek final solutions?

Mitigate the need to Shore-Up

In the political environment, moving to action is much more complex than we would expect. The community leader that is seeking solutions to community issues and problem must first recognize how political leaders will view their demands. Any request for relief from an existing policy or a request to institute any new political intervention will be weighed in terms of threat potential. The nature of the threat will be assessed in terms of the probability of causing significant tension to cause political disequilibrium. The presence of disequilibrium immediately forces a political leader to engage in Shoring-Up activity.

If the threat is viewed as a legitimate threat to political power, the Shoring-Up action is likely to be overt, confrontational and seek efforts to totally neutralize the community's ability to oppose the political leader. To avoid this reaction, a single issue community problem needs to be linked to issues that support the political agenda. The interjection of a new demand has to be framed in such a way that its solution benefits of the overall political agenda and the ability to fulfill the vision. While relatively easy to say, the implementation of this approach is difficult.

However the difficulty has a tendency to lessen when community leaders take the big picture or systems approach and can assist the political leader in "seeing" the big picture benefit. Community leaders need to also be aware that in picking issues for action, certain prerequisites are necessary.

First and foremost, initiatives must have a base of support that warrants attention and that a lack of attention would spark widespread community participation in the resolution (Mattessich and Monsey 1997). Without this condition, political leaders would view the situation as not being capable or creating tension or eventual disequilibrium.

Maintain the political equilibrium

The key in not raising the level of community tension is to have a complete understanding of what is going on and what the political leader believes is the current situation. As one political activist community leader told me;

"I have always been stubborn and hard-headed and tenacious but it has been very useful to me... When you know the facts before you ask for help, it helps you a whole lot to proceed to ask the next step...anyway, finding out the information -- and In working with all our elected officials, ...I found that elected officials do not know all the answers and, in fact, you have to find the answers to give to them so they can help you. In some ways they are dependent upon you knowing stuff they don't"

The community leaders in Hill Top and Lake Village took great effort in getting all the information and sharing that information with the political leaders. This was a method in which the potential opposition was now viewed as helpful in framing the issue. It is interesting to view the lack of information or misinformation that some elected leaders have and believe. Community groups that can give political leaders vital and factual information immediately change their positional view from potential threat to potential ally. The exchange below illustrates this point. The community was seeking assistance in building highway sound barriers. The same community leader expressed the following;

"We worked with the Congresswoman at the time to explain to her that she had bad information -- when we first wrote her a letter, she wrote us a letter back in which she was strictly repeating what state highway had told her. We were looking for somebody who could actually get mad and upset like we were, and that inaccurate information she got from the state put her in a position of knowing that she also had been lied to. Now the Governor had announced the week before that there wouldn't be any more sound barriers... So we presented our correct information to the Congresswoman and two weeks later she had a press conference to announce that, yes, in fact, these barriers would be put into place."

This illustrates that by taking the approach of helping a political official with valid information, the community leaders were able to supply an opportunity for the political leader to have a very public victory which assisted in solidifying the leader's power. What could have been a confrontation between community leaders and the elected officials was averted. This eliminated the tension and kept the political environment in equilibrium. In this case the community leader was careful not to allow a situation where they were closed out by a fortification of political coalitions.

Structure of the equilibrium system

It is essential that before any overt action is attempted by a community leader, that the elements required to be in equilibrium within the community system are known. The ability to know which individuals and which groups are the natural allies of the political leader is a useful piece of information in seeking to maintain equilibrium. Having a basic understanding of their issues and agenda will help establish the root of the political leader's power and influence. Knowing this prevents inadvertent threats to this political coalition that helps maintain the leader's position and power. An ideal situation could be established if the community leader who is seeking to influence public policy, could find a way to link the goals of the in power coalition to the desired new policy initiative.

If on the other hand, the political intervention sought is in current opposition to the goals and desires of the coalition groups, then community leaders need to address attempts at getting support from those groups before reaching out to the political leader. The pre-emptive approach will keep equilibrium. My experience in this area has been that to get potential opposition groups to change a stated position is not an easy task. The best approach is to address areas where all groups can potentially agree and then move towards compromise on the areas of disagreement. This process, often referred to a "chunking", seeks to divide the issue into its smallest actionable parts then find a course of action on this element of the overall problem. By gaining a series of small agreements, the community leader is now in a position to seek the political leader's interventions. Even if the coalition groups have not totally agreed, the level of opposition's resistance is low enough, as to not threaten equilibrium.

CHAPTER

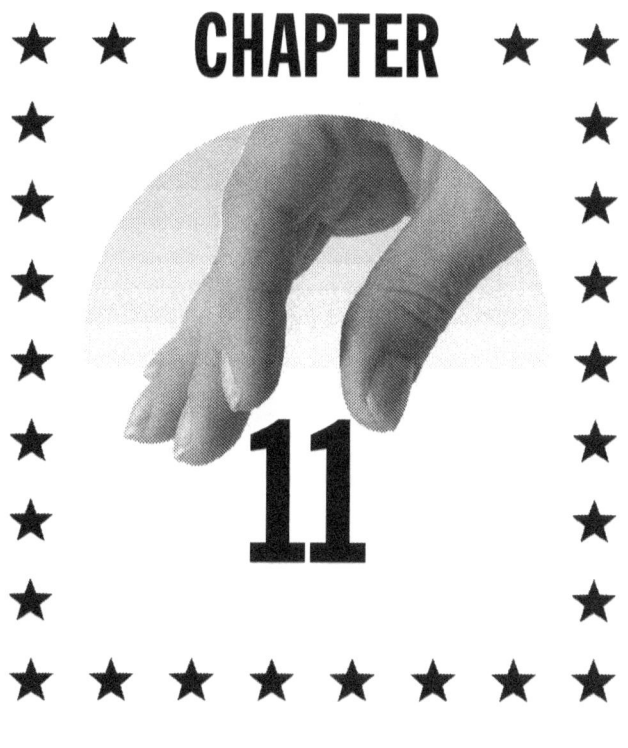

11

Just Do It!

Chapter 11

Just Do It!

Often we hear the term "manage change". As I have mentioned earlier, the political process is messy, turbulent and chaotic. I'm not sure that it is possible to manage that situation but I am convinced that an effective process can be utilized to put the elements of change in motion. This type of activity is more of a leadership issue than one of management. To take the lead in political change requires leadership that motivates and even inspires.

The first step is to simply step in and evaluate your resources. Examine your potential for building coalitions and a political powerbase. An effective program for political change can not be waged from the outside. Only those who are willing to venture into the community process can hope to accomplish anything.

Next, be prepared to articulate a clear statement of mission. A defined purpose is essential. The simpler the mission statement the better it is understood. "Defeat proposition…or eliminate council district…" is much more powerful than some long winded attempt to specify all the issues.

The building of a team of political activists is the next step in the process. Use community forums to discuss your views and strategy. Visit the community association. Use the media if you are working on a potentially hot issue. Use anything that garners attention. Bottom line is that you need a critical mass of supporters.

Lone wolves may have their uses but facilitating change is not one of them. A political action team will need a variety of skills. These include political skills in navigating the social system of the community and the power structure. Some have said the lower the stakes the more political it becomes. The change agent needs to navigate past the petty politics that can derail the effort, but they had better understand the issues and the forces seeking to defeat their efforts.

Other team skills required include analytical skills. Change agents and leaders must have the ability to analyze situations. In politics in particular, guessing won't cut it. A politician will immediately recognize if he is standing in an abundance of fertilizer. He has become a pro at manufacturing the stuff and knows it when he smells it.

While insight is valuable and on occasion offers nuggets of brilliance, it alone is difficult to sell and almost always impossible to defend. A rational well argued analysis can most certainly be ignored by others but it can never be successfully defeated on its merit.

From an operations perspective, two skill sets are needed. These are the ability to develop workflow and systems understanding. The recruitment of followers to your cause and the ability to inundate the political targets with memos, information and other communications requires the ability to organized a workflow and generate massive output.

You need to know how to disrupt and overburden the political system to get attention.

Additionally, the ability of financial analysis is needed to allocate and understand what needs to be done to replenish resources. The milk of political life is money or access to the resources it can buy. Your attempts to create change are further enhanced if word processing, computer systems knowledge, and good business skills are available.

Angela Bischoff and Tooker Gomberg from Greenspiration.org offer the following as the "Ten Commandments for political change". As they put it; "Ten Commandments for changing the world": They rightfully assert, "Changing the world is a blast. It's all the more achievable if you have some basic skills, and lots of chutzpah."

I have utilized their basic concepts and have added my own commentary and interpretation of their principles to offer the following:

1. You have got to Believe.

Have hope, passion and confidence that valuable change can and does happen because individuals take bold initiative. You must be totally convinced that you will prevail no matter how long it takes you will ultimately win. Don't put a definite time for your winning. If you reach your time point and have not achieved victory, then you will become discouraged. Just resolve to persist and see your effort to the end no matter how long it takes.

2. Challenge Authority.

Don't be afraid to question authority. Authority should be earned, not appointed. The "experts" are often proven wrong — they used to believe that the earth was flat. You don't have to be an expert to have a valuable opinion or to speak out on an issue. I also suggest you always challenge what is considered conventional wisdom in politics. Conventional wisdom will always tell you to give up. You can't prevail. We have too many examples of citizens groups prevailing to think that you can not win.

3. Know the System.

The system perpetuates itself. Use the tools you have. The telephone is the most underrated. The internet can be of great value for research as well. Learn how decisions are made. How is the bureaucracy structured? Who are the key players? What do they look like? Where do they eat lunch? Go there and talk with them. Get to know their executive assistants. Attend public meetings. The goal is to make the existing system work for you. You can't change it so you must learn how to work it.

4. Take Action

Do something — anything is better than nothing. Bounce your idea around with friends, and then act. Start small, but think big. Organize public events. Distribute handbills. Involve youth. It's easier to ask for forgiveness after you ruffle the political feathers of your targets after you act rather than to ask for some bureaucratic overseer's permission. Just do it! Be flexible. Roll with the punches and allow yourself to change tactics mid-stream. Think laterally. Don't get hung-up on money matters; some of the best actions have no budget. The object is to create some environmental discomfort and to breakup the current political equilibrium.

5. Use the media.

Letters to the Editor of your local newspaper are read by thousands. Stage a dramatic event and invite the media. They love an event that gives them an interesting angle or good photo opportunity. If you are looking to spontaneously generate a crowd of people to show real or simulated strength then by all means think of ways to bypass the mainstream media with email and World Wide Web to get the word out about your issue and to network. Create stress for the opposition.

6. Build Alliances.

Seek out your common allies such as other community associations, seniors, youth groups, labor, businesses, etc. and work with them to establish support. The system wins through Divide and Conquer, so do the opposite! Network ideas, expertise and issues through email lists. Celebrate your successes with others. Even if the alliance is short term and on one issue, learn to embrace their needs to advance your cause.

7. Apply Constant Pressure.

Persevere — it drives those in power crazy. Be as creative as possible in getting your issues and perspective heard. Use the media, phone your politicians, send letters and faxes with graphics and images. Be concise. Bend the Administration's ear when you attend public meetings. Take notes. Ask specific questions, and give a deadline for when you expect a response. Stay in their faces. As I stated earlier, politicians depend on your frustration and fatigue causing you to abandon the issue.

8. Preach an Alternative.

There is one basic truth in seeking change. Being against something is not nearly enough to cause change. New ideas, new passion, and new approaches to old problems are what will cause change. It is vital that you propose and articulate intelligent alternatives to the status quo. Inspire people with well thought out, attractive visions of how things can be better. Use actual examples, what's been tried, where and how it works. Do your homework. Get the word out, and create visual representations. Be positive and hopeful.

9. Learn from your Mistakes and those of others.

You're going to make mistakes; we all do. The key is trying not repeating them. Critique in a positive way – your efforts, the movement, and the opposition. What works, and why? What isn't working? What works and do more of the same. Study what other groups have done to be successful and study why others groups failed.

10. Take Care of Yourself and Each Other

Maintain balance. Political campigns are grueling both physically and mentally. Remember to eat well and get regular exercise and ample sleep. Winners learn how to avoid burnout by delegating tasks, sharing responsibility, and maintaining an open process. Be sensitive to your fellow activist and help them maintain a balance. Most of all this process is fun. The world will go on no matter the outcome of your mission. Have fun. It's the only way to hold it all together. As much as possible, surround yourself with others (both at work and at play) who share your vision so you can build camaraderie, solidarity and support

Political wheels do not move without a sufficient push that is often little more than the illusion of a building political opposition group. The essence of tension formation and the creation of disequilibrium stem from agitation.

Pressure Groups

In the process of forcing political change through coercion, negotiation and compromise much of this activity is processed through what would have to be considered pressure groups. Within modern social communities, pressure groups are found among the numerous voluntary associations.

Almost every interest in society, almost every element in bodies and political leaders. The principal sources of legislative activity historically have been the directive or planning urged by political leaders feeling the impact or perceived pressure from pressure groups.

We can see the development and evolution of pressure groups from the past in the form of groups from the legal profession, the clergy, the landowners, the merchants, and the leaders of localities. Modern pressure-groups have grown in close relation to the various political party systems. When there are many parties, a number of such interest groups can be absorbed into the party system that best addresses their issues in a manner that is acceptable to the parties involved. With our two party system, such pressure groups are typically independent organizations.

Typically the problem of pressure groups becomes almost inextricable from the general study of the political parties, but I want to emphasisize here, that party alignment or affiliation is not necessary and in fact may work against political activity on the local or community level.

American society has traditionally been relatively free of class consciousnesses in that talent and hard work can allow one to pass through or to various social classes. This is demonstrated endlessly by the public affirmation of the "in" group versus the "out" group and the rise and fall of differentiated power groups over the political history of the country. The politician has been an individualist, footloose and free to bargain and willing to deal with a variety of opposing groups. In fact, political survival demands this kind of bargaining with the power brokers. Furthermore, the American economy is tremendously diversified, the population exceedingly heterogeneous, and the political structure greatly decentralized and integrated. The formal structure of the government cannot reflect faithfully any large part of the interests, which must seek informal ways of influencing the government.

Three Levels of Organization Pressure

From the beginning, It should be understood that the ability to bring the pressure to bear on any particular social target takes work, coordination and the willingness and the ability to build coalitions of groups with a common goal and directed energy. Even if the formed coalitions are ones of convenience and single issued for one moment in time, they are essential to the successful outcome of a political action.

As such this section will help distinguish the degrees of organization in the typical citizen pressure groups. Beginning with the sporadic attempts of individuals to influence the government, I will move on to discuss the pressure group as it has developed in the American political process.

On each level of organization, I will be concerned with appraising the social groups producing the pressure, the amount and the impact of such pressure, and the techniques of the groups.

Individual's Influence in Politics

Any Analysis of voting behavior of any population around the world that has free and open election processes shows that economic and social interests rule the way many people vote. I personally feel comfortable with the notion that most people are obviously motivated by their own immediate interests when they cast their vote. There does seem to be some relationship between the way people vote and their economic and social levels.

Many people vote the way they think will benefit most immediately their pockets or their particular religious, nationality, local, or racial groups. Furthermore, those voters that are active in politics, generally seek their own personal interests through the political party.

Any Individual Can Exert Influence

While admittedly difficult, even individuals outside of a political party can sometimes exert enough pressure to win a personal battle with the political process. These are the politicos who, without belonging to continuously organized groups, still can exert pressure on the government over and above their party or voting activities. Among this group would be individuals who seek favors of some sort from the government. Typically these range from seeking an exception to a municipal zoning ordinances all the way to influencing the granting of a contract for state or national government construction projects. People who can extract these favors are most likely those who have developed political influence through their ability to supply either funds or votes to the political process. In reality that is not the venue in which the average citizen activist operates.

Others Among the individual influencers would be the individual advocates of "causes," ranging from the construction of a municipal swimming pool to the establishment of a national bird sanctuary. The number of such persons, contrary to popular belief, is not infinite. The active public, we have pointed out, is not large. A single citizen, inspired by an intense selfish or altruistic purpose, can exert an influence greatly disproportionate to his numerical influence as one.

Most politicians who have had any considerable experience in public life can name specific individuals in their constituencies who are intensely interested in some aspect of politics and who persist in making their influence felt. If this influence is not supported by the ability to deliver the elements of political success such as money and votes; then it is tied to one ability to be a public pain in the ass. For example, almost every politician who has had a hand in any legislation concerning the conservation or destruction of wild life will have heard from one active woman who has devoted much of her adult life to influencing public attitudes towards wildlife conservation. The harsh reality is that she is likely to gain favorable action for fear that she is able to build some power-base to assult the power and position of the politician.

Whatever the political jurisdiction, so few people pay attention to the workings of government that anyone who will spend a few hours a month on some subject of government over a long period of time can become a leader of opinion and action.

This is true not only of party politics but also of activity in any one of the hundreds of areas in which the government is doing something- the tax rate on personal property, the problems of sewage disposal or the construction of a superhighway.

However, I would be remiss if I didn't illuminate the odds of successful outcomes with a one person campaign. The probability is small. The way an individual beats those odds is through building support among groups that can exert the appropriate pressure to the politician. Sometimes the most unlikely of coalitions can be brought together for a single issue and become very powerful.

"The wheel that squeaks, gets the grease." A mere handful of individuals, raising a clamor that cannot be stilled by constitutional means, can embarrass, badger, and even control a politician, a party, or an agency of government. Citizens who discover this fact for the first time are as astonished as the small boy who enters a great cavern and hears the resounding echo of his shouts. A few people are permanently unbalanced by the shock. They unfortunately become experts on everything, and appear at every stage of the legislative process, as drunk with power as ever a government official might be. Their entrance on the scene of a meeting, hearing, or conference brings shudders to those acquainted with them.

Pressures can be good or bad

Unfortunately, no formula can say which of these various individual pressures is good and which is bad. Pressure is neither good nor bad. In many cases it depends on where you stand. One can influence the government to his own benefit; but one can also influence the government to relieve famine in India. This is as true of individuals as well as the social groups discussed below. The desire to be a political activist must be determined in one's own mind. The extent to which one can exert pressure depends on individual passion and commitment.

I will discuss how someone chooses to become an activist in later pages.

Nowhere is it more apparent than in the debate over pressure politics that most people consider their own ideas legitimate and true and those of their opponents illegitimate and false. Just look at the fervor over such political positions as pro life versus pro choice in the abortion debate. The mere fact that a person advocates reforms on behalf of others does not argue in itself for his goodness.

Building a Power Base

John Kretzmann and John McKnight in their book "Building Communities from the Inside Out" (Institute for Policy Research, Northwestern University, 1993) offer a number of interesting observations in the process of building community actions that are quite appropriate in the process of building political power and influence for change. I have liberally borrowed some of their core concepts and modified some of their concepts for this section to relate them to dealing with and creating political power for citizen groups.

The first and most compelling observation is that most communities and I add special interest groups seeking change; begin the process by citing all the needs, deficiencies, and problems as the central focus of all activity. As an alternative and I think a more positive approach is to examine the capacity of the initiating group's assets to cause and effect change. In short, what is your current capacity and what can you do now with that capacity. It becomes the basis for a successful strategy of Incrementalism.

How do you eat an elephant? One bite at a time! If you can find others to help, then you build capacity to consume the elephant at a faster rate with an enhanced likelihood of success.

In the community action model in which the participants offer a laundry list of things that are deficient, we basically ask those in power to respond to our needs and become dependent upon there interest and goodwill. Communities invite themselves to become "clients" of the power holder totally dependent on their action or lack of action.

The real problem with this approach is that it puts the community or community leadership in the battle for limited resources. This is establishing the group or community as a "victim class" that seeks to have others do for them. The truth is that those resources will always go to the groups that have the "capacity" to exert political influence through control of assets needed by the politician. In this scenario, the politicians become the "client" of those who can control the assets. I think that the situation of fighting for resources allocation based on greatest need is summed best below:

★ Special interest groups and communities that represent themselves as endless list of demands accented by needs, deficiencies leads to fragmented efforts to provide solutions. It also denies the basic community wisdom to solve problems.

★ Targeting resources based on needs tends to direct those resources to service providers in the favor of the politicians instead of the community.

★ Providing resources based on a need basis, underlines the dependency need of the group on outside resources. This produces a cycle of dependency that requires that things get continuously worst in order to gain resources each year. A side effect for your consideration here is that politicians need these dependency groups in place so that supports and votes are available to keep the handouts coming.

★ Obtaining resources on a needs basis only highlights the ineffectiveness of group leadership when those resources go elsewhere. It undermines the ability of community activist leaders to seek solutions within the existing capacity of the group.

★ Dependence on a needs policy structure insures that communities and special interest groups will operate in survival mode, not an aggressive problem solving force
★ Communities and groups in survival mode are never instruments of political change.

The alternative approach forces communities and community leaders to think in terms of their strengths not their weaknesses. Every individual and group has a unique combination of assets. We have a tendency to marginalize those with limited capacity when if combined with all other capacity would add significantly to the potential skill and power base. (John Kretzmann and John McKnight, 1993)

If we just look at the institutional resources within a community we can see how this works. Local institutions such as areas businesses, schools, parks, libraries, hospitals and community colleges make up a typical community. Independently these institutions have tremendous resources in terms of talent, cash, facilities etc. If all of these were harnessed for one purpose, the focus becomes what can we accomplish as apposed to what do we need.

The community institutions joined by the citizens associations like churches, cultural groups and block clubs adds to the resources. We then add in the resources of individuals such as, income, the enthusiasm and energy of youth, the skills of artists and communicators, the wisdom and experience of the elderly and even the limited capacity of what we refer to "labeled people" who suffer from social and medical problems can all add to capacity.

This asset based, internally focused and relationship driven force is in the best position to effect social or political change.

Mapping community and organizational assets

As a beginning it is important to remind the reader that as citizens seeking to influence public policy or political process we are endowed with capacity and gifts. If we go as clients of the system, we are endowed with needs and deficiencies. In other words don't approach building powerful opposition organizations from a position of weakness. This is not a "hat in hand" approach to asking for more.

Mapping begins with citizens leaders conducting an inventory of capacity. The task is to identify individuals and their particular capacities, institutions and their unique ability and capacity, and citizen association.

Next, community leaders will need to identify and or establish a method of communications with and among the elements. If engaged in community building, all kinds of skills and commitments are useful. Capacity to do construction, provide child care, provide meeting space, transportation to and from meetings, equipment repair and maintenance is all useful in providing community capacity to accomplish a mission.

In the process of trying to influence public policy or political change, we might seek capacity for facilitating meetings, visiting other community groups, provide phone banks, write letters, or call in to radio talk shows as examples. For any of these to operate as an effective force for change, citizen leaders must build complete and effective capacity maps that demonstrate existing or potential linkages. The communication system must be developed and implemented between the community elements. In this way of combined or joined capacity, an effective coalition of assets can be directed at policy makers to insure the attention of the targeted group.

Open communication and dialogue between the community elements is essential. The use of open meetings, community newsletters and combined social and community events leads to team building and the strengthening of the coalitions formed.

When this coalition of assets is targeted in this manner, they also implicitly announce control and influence over the resources, the people, and institutions that can deliver money and votes. Politicians must have access to these assets in order to maintain power, control and influence.

Community Action

There are long term consequences for citizens and political activists who fail to recognize the behaviors of Political Shoring-Up. In the short run, we have social issues that are not addressed because political leaders can and do seek shelter within the established coalitions that hold the key to their political power.

The long term effect of Shoring-Up behavior is that the real causes of social problems and conflict are never directly addressed. The use of Shoring-Up behaviors puts into play other forces that have an impact on the community. Since the local community is a working system, any change in the inputs or changes in the processing elements. The adjustment of any input will change the dynamics of the system. Shoring-Up behavior as a result of community action is the conscious effort to push difficult or politically unattractive decisions to some time in the future.

It skillfully avoids the political fallout associated with politically incorrect solutions and in some cases can push the decision off to another political office holder in the future. However the use of short term Shoring-Up activity will effect the relationships within the system.

The Shoring-Up approach is designed to only address the symptomatic consequences of some underlying cause. The use of Shoring-Up interventions adversely affects final solutions in that the pressure within the social system is lessened to the point that short term equilibrium is established. This state, in-turn, eliminates the need to find the ultimate solution at the present time, even when it is evident that the problem will return in the future. The need to "fix" social security so that it remains a viable and solvent program is a prime example of this tactic.

The economist, Keynes, commented that economics viewed in the long run is not relevant because in "the long run we're all dead". Politics is similar in that in the long run, political leaders will have moved on and have left office long before the repercussions of inaction show up. In exploring the adverse effect of prolonged use of Shoring-Up behaviors it was advantageous to view this political activity in context of a local community in which it occurs.

A revisit to the studied communities in my case study helps to illustrate the consequences of Shoring-Up. Communities like all organizations are systems and therefore a systems analysis approach is merited in exploring this case study because the consequences of short term limited approaches can be examined within the data. Through observation and analysis of the circumstances within Hill Top and Lakeside, I demonstrated that several system archetype models offer the best explanation and illustration of the consequences of Shoring-Up actions in reducing the treat of political tension, disequilibrium and threat of mission derailment. Any disruption to the state of equilibrium is a disruption of the function of the political and the community systems.

The Lakeside community example from the interview below illustrates how a potential racial issue was neutralized by refocusing the problem and gaining the support of the police, elected officials, the business community and most importantly of all the full community. Once the issue of race was neutralized, all sides could find common ground to resolve the issue of crime, unsupervised youth, and the lack of other appropriate activities for teens.

According to a community association president, *"There was an issue about a skating rink property that turned loose about 300 kids at 11:00 at night, who were doing some major, serious property damage within the commercial area. Skate Land on Orchard Tree Lane was at the center of the problem. The community wanted some controls or restrictions on the operation. Basically we wanted the operator and the county police to work together to give more supervision at closing time. The police and the operator announced a tighter security and curfew program. Immediately the black community leaders took offense since most of the patrons were black youths and what was presented was the Community Council was withdrawn because an African-American Preacher had threatened the Council with a suit for being anti-black. So here we have a threat from the black community...I was raised by a mother from Ohio; my father was from New York City and grew up in Texas. I never, in any way thought that there was any real difference between people; people were people. And have found that to be true all my life and I accept people as they accept me. There's (sic) people I don't like no matter what color, there's people I love no matter what color. So when the threat was that the community was reacting in a racial way I started looking at what was being done. Hey guys, this is economic. When you have $23,000 dollars worth of property damage in one night, when you have a McDonalds that is torn up, when you have 24-hour businesses like Dunkin' Donuts and 7-11, and whatever, closing because of this problem, this is not a racial issue, this is an economic issue that is going to destroy our community if we don't get something done. So it's not -- you have to be either brave enough or stupid enough to stand up for what you believe, and convince people that you are doing this for the right reason. And if you make sense and you are doing it for the right reason, most people will accept it."*

In effect, what this community leader was able to accomplish by reframing the issue was to ease the potential by actually eliminating the sources of tension. The problem was segmented or "chunked" to three smaller issues.

★ First, that vandalism was a problem that should be addressed.
★ Second, the problem was detrimental to community business interest.
★ Third, large numbers of youths needed alternative community activity which provided supervision after the skate rink closed.

All groups and political coalitions could agree on the preceding issues and eventually on the resolution of the problem without the political leader needing to expend any political capital on getting the solution. In fact this outcome allowed the political leader to accumulate political capital.

CHAPTER

12

Your Role as a
Community Leader

Chapter 12

Your Role as a Community Leader

One purpose of this book is hopefully to encourage the emergence of more active citizens - people motivated by an interest in public issues, and a desire to make a difference beyond their own private lives. Active citizens are a great untapped resource, and citizenship is a quality to be nurtured.

Active community associations or loosely organized citizens groups find that they can find better and more efficient ways of tackling large public issues by "chunking" the issues into more digestible components that are easier for political leaders to accept. It is the process of gaining on large issues through incrementally initiated strategies.

When people become involved in their neighborhoods, they can become a potent force for dealing with local problems. Through coordinated planning, research and action, they can accomplish what individuals working alone most likely could not have accomplished.

When people decide they are going to be part of the solution, local problems start getting solved. When they actually begin to work with other individuals, schools, associations, businesses, and government service providers, there is no limit to what they can accomplish.

Citizens can make cities work better because they understand their own neighborhoods better than anyone else. Giving them some responsibility for looking after their part of town is a way of effectively addressing local preferences and priorities. Understandably, boosting citizen participation improves livability. It is no coincidence that Portland, Oregon - a city with a tradition of working in partnership with neighborhoods - regularly receives the highest score for livability of any U.S. city.

Cities are sources of potential conflict, between government and citizens, between different citizens groups, and between citizens and special interests such as real estate developers. Some well done studies:

* **The Rebirth of Urban Democracy;** Jeff Berry, Kent Portney, Ken Thomson; Brookings, Washington, DC, 1993;
* **The Quickening of America,** Frances Moore Lappe and Paul Martin DuBois, Jossey-Bass, San Francisco, 1994;
* **Bowling Alone, The collapse and revival of American community**, Robert Putnam, Simon & Schuster, NY, 2000;
* **Reinventing Government**, David Osborne & Ted Gaebler, Penguin Paperbacks, 1993;
* **Busting Bureaucracy: How to Conquer Your Organization's Worst Enemy** Kenneth Johnston, Business One Irwin, 1993; have shown that greater citizen participation in civic affairs can reduce all of these sources of conflict and more importantly demonstrate that organized citizens can be the catalyst for change in the face of stiff politician's resolve to do otherwise.

When citizens get together at the neighborhood level, they generate a number of remarkable side effects. One of these is strengthened democracy. In simple terms, democracy means that the people decide. Political scientists describe our system of voting every few years but otherwise leaving everything up to government as weak democracy. In a weak democracy, citizens have no role, no real part in decision-making between elections. Experts assume responsibility for deciding how to deal with important public issues.

The great movement of the last decades of the twentieth century has been a drive toward stronger democracy in corporations, institutions and governments. In many cities this has resulted in the formal recognition of neighborhood groups as a link between people and municipal government, and a venue for citizen participation in decision-making between elections.

And finally, Active citizens can help to create a sense of community connected to place and a sense of empowerment as to the ability to control the destiny of both the individual and community.

Community involvement and Public Policy

The decisions and non-decisions made by our political leaders form and implement the public policy that dominates our quality of lives. The impact that public policy has upon individual life and our ability to make our own decisions can not be ignored.

The interjection of new policy, whether it is an overt directed action or a default position through a non-decision, without doubt changes the dynamics within a community and changes how the system operates. Any change has an impact on the individual's ability to control individual destiny.

In the real world, "public policy is whatever governments choose to do or not do…they regulate conflict,…they organize society to carry on conflict against others…they distribute… symbolic rewards and material services to members; and they extract money…in the form of taxes."(Dye, 2002. p.1)

Political leaders and those charged with the conservation of community wellness have in selected cases greatly underestimated the impact that their political actions. This is true not out of a total disregard for doing things the right way, but as a result of not understanding the dynamics of the community. That is for every action, there is a counter action. It is in this way that we end up with the formerly unseen unintended consequences.

It can be demonstrated that changes in public policy without regard to the impact on the total community system can threaten the continued viability of residential communities. Too often our political leaders are looking for ways to avoid conflict and political imbalance. Therefore, they establish public policy for political expediency in an effort to shore-up an endangered political position (Patnode. 2004).

It has been demonstrated that seemingly unrelated political policy decisions can have an impact on later actions or influence the behavior of others in ways that evolve as unintended consequences of the original political policy.

As part of my research for this book, I examined how families decide to relocate from one community to another. The main difference between communities that loose people and those that attract people can be tied to how political decisions within a community either contributed to its deterioration or made it more desirable by creating policy actions that contributed to the living environment.

Of course the family decision process to move from one community to another is complex. Typical factors for consideration are economic, social, cultural and geographic and expectations for continued community stability. Each of these elements will carry an individual weight based on the needs and experience of family members, but all will in some way contribute to the choice of a new community. Not surprisingly, families of child bearing age take into consideration the quality of the community schools (Rusk. 1999. P.259)

In a community going through a traditional life cycle, it has been shown that existing residents with children now grown recognize the importance in maintaining viable schools. Without good schools, communities have difficulty in attracting new younger residents to replace older residents who choose to move into more appropriate accommodations.

Typically, perspective new community members are seeking a school that is judged to be equal or superior to that of schools in the former location. For families, this becomes a key element in their choice. As such, political and community leaders are accustomed to reacting to any negative factors in community schools. However, this imperative to give constituents visible action on problems is for the sole purpose of lessening political tension.

The willingness to use patchwork solutions is in fact disruptive to the functioning of the community system. Community development and preservation are continuous challenges for both local governments and community leaders. Often the multitude of problems faced by community leaders in maintaining the proper balance of the community system become overwhelming, causing a decline in the overall "wellness" of the community. When this imbalance becomes noticeable to these leaders, they seek actions that limit the distress. Trust me when I tell you; the focus is on the short term without regard for long term consequences.

Such actions seem to be evidence of a political survival first mentality without seeking social solutions.

This failure to consider and understand the complex nature of social problems can result in new problems of greater magnitude than the original concern because of unintended and unforeseen consequences.

The role of community leaders in seeking to gain political leadership support for community interventions can be tied to a series of actions. The first and the basis for all community action strategy is the collection of information. All too often, individuals seek political action based solely on emotions or opinions. Political leaders even sympathetic to a plea, can only respond to information that holds substance, supports action, and is believed by the majority of constituents and is consistent with the beliefs and the goals of the leader.

This is true even if the information poses a threat to the political agenda. In my interview with a community association leader, the following comments illustrate how community leaders view the importance of information and knowledge of the system in which they operate.

"Sometimes I cringe when I go to hearings or I listen to people at Zoning Hearings or Community Input Meetings... because people come out with a very self-centered, self-focused viewpoint how they feel about things. They don't see the bigger picture. They're automatically in the defensive mode, and you really get nowhere that way, because everybody automatically sets up boundaries and blockades; they don't want to listen to each other. And that's -- people -- it's very hard -- it took me intensive study, three years, to find out how the development process works; to understand zoning code, to understand what BL, BR, BM means, what the uses are allowed. It's something like 1,500 pages. I mean you had to sit there and read it, and highlight, and underline, and make margin notes to understand what this is. And it's still -- it is still so convoluted and hard to understand that a lot of times even your attorneys and engineers don't even understand what the actual code is. What isn't used on an everyday daily basis, you have to go back and review. Before every hearing I have to go back and review."

Communication

The other basic role of the community leader is that of communication and the dissemination of the information collected. Communication is critical in the success of community request for political intervention. Several leaders expressed in conversations that; tell everyone everything philosophy works much more for your cause than against it.

The following excerpt is an example of how one of my interviewees handles the communication role.

"I got the newsletter going out trying to get information -- communication out to the community, as well as set up an identity to the area by our elected officials. Here we are, who we are, they get a newsletter on their desk everyday -- I mean once a month. The Business Association came in kind of hot and heavy. A lot of the officers were in banking. There's (sic) a lot of transfers in banking; they go from one bank to another or go this bank branch to another bank branch, so the Business Association kind of took a down turn in 1996. We gave a proposal to the County in a request for grant funding for newsletter coverage, as well as for the position of a co-executive director. The idea was to get business and community working together; not as two separate entities but together."

Understanding the issues on all sides

There is an old axiom that is very true in politics. That is "know your enemy". That is particularly true when you are looking for political favor and others have the potential to offer opposition to that favor. Often, this requires a preemptive action on the part of community leaders to neutralize the opposition. It is time to seek an understanding of the basis for any opposition. This is particularly true if the opposition has historically been supportive of the current political leadership.

It will be necessary to seek accommodation if at all possible because without either gaining their support or getting opposition to a neutral position; no positive action can happen. The reality of political life is that politicians are beholding to those who support their positions and vision and provide the financial resources to mount political campaigns.

A community association leader offered the following example.

"When seeking to organize some renters, a Coordinator for Community conservation once told me, you can't do that; why can't we I

asked? This is what is needed in this area. Well, you see, they make a lot of political contributions to our elected politicians. The owners of those properties don't want tenants to actually be organized."
This required a redirection at discovering the issues that landlord's need to resolve. In this case the effort failed and political opposition stopped an initiative to organize renters within the community associations.

Get people involved
To have any impact in the political process, community leaders must use many of the same tools and techniques utilized by political leaders. Building coalitions and support groups is an important aspect of gaining political favor. The key however in implementing an action, is to avoid Shoring-Up behaviors that block the prospects for a final solution.

Any coalition built needs to be linked in some way to the same coalitions that support the political leadership. The goal is to become a needed element within the quest of the political vision. It is the process used in the martial arts of using the force that is directed against your goal versus opposing the force. Even opposing forces can agree on something that allows them to combine their collective strengths to achieve a goal. My interview with a community leader offered the following observation.

"We felt there's always strength in numbers and if you get what say two organizations usually parallel each other or even fight or have adversarial positions together, if you get people together focusing on the same goal, that strength becomes even greater"
Other approaches often used by community leaders, is an attempt to broaden the base of support. Community leaders actively seek support from other unrepresented groups which may be of interest or concern to the political leader. The broader the bases of support coupled with facts that sup-

port a position makes it easier for a political leader to offer help without the need to Shore-Up any other positions.

Solution cost/benefit

In the political environment every action, gesture, or concession is done with a quid pro quo attached. Community leaders can not expect positive reactions from political leaders without first recognizing that they need to eliminate any perception of a threat. This requires the ability to offer a political cost benefit analysis to the political leadership. This helps assess the positive results of outcomes. These must the political vision, contributes to maintaining equilibrium, solidifies political power, and overall offers greater political benefit than the cost of any political capital.

Long term approach

The most difficult behavior that a community leader is forced to adopt is the reorientation from dealing with the immediate problem to a focus on taking a bigger picture and long term approach. It is understandable that people seek to lessen a current discomfort. The benefits of a final solution need to be convincingly sold to them. They must also understand the long term ramifications of any proposed short term interventions.

The long term approach also eliminates the immediate possibility of creating a threat to the political equilibrium. Without this threat, it is more probable that political leaders will not feel compelled to engage in the stop-gap behaviors. This in turn offers a greater opportunity for a final or long term solutions instead of a political tactical diversion.

Passion

Based on my observations and discussions with community Leaders, it appears to me that community leadership is hard work. Quite often it is non-paid. It requires perseverance and the ability in organizing people. You must work at getting people on the same page. You accomplish that by making a convincing argument using facts and good statistics. When seeking political favors, you must have an absolute conviction that your community doesn't just want something but deserves it. This requires a personal commitment and passion for winning.

Shoring-Up defenses

It is possible that attempts to thwart Shoring-Up behavior will not work. That for some undiscovered reason the political leader can only respond with Shoring-Up behaviors for fear of alienating any support base. In this circumstance, it is better to recognize the behavior in order to mount the appropriate political pressure on the problem for which redress is sought.

The key to mounting an offensive response to Shoring-Up is in recognizing a political leaders resistance to taking definitive action towards a final solution. My experience and observations tell me that any political initiative taken by the political leadership, that is a diversion or a delay to making a final solution decision, is usually an indication that disequilibrium is expected.

Community leaders placed in this situation must first seek to neutralize possible opposition coalitions. Traditionally, these coalitions will seek to limit the community and its leadership from forming credible opposition to the political leader. The reality of the situation at this point is that community leaders have two choices. The first is to seek accommodation and attempt to relieve tension and potential disequilibrium. The second is to prepare for confrontation and the creation of opposition groups to either change the will of the political leader and their supporters or in a democratic society seek to remove or replace a leader that can not maintain the majority support

As examples of this we can revisit Hilltop and Lakeside. A variety of typical community ills had surfaced. At issue was a decaying community. Through the collective efforts of community activists, community associations, businesses, churches, social organizations and use of the press; this coalition was able to find a way to decrease crime, increase home ownership, reinvigorate the retail commercial base and improve failing schools. While admittedly the efforts to date are not complete, the collective power of the coalition was enough to pose a threat to existing political office holders to the point that it was safer for the politicians to make changes rather than face possible loss of office.

Some Keys to a building a powerful organization

Jim Collins, in his book "Good to Great", offers a new way to look at organizations that I think translates very well to building political action groups.

Collins, as we did above, takes the approach of using your capacity to accomplish goals as apposed to setting a goal then go fine the assets and capacity needed to reach the goal. The basic concept he proposes is that we should view any group or organization as a bus with seats. The leader's role and challenge is to get the right people on the bus and through understanding their capacity, have them in the right seat. Once the bus is full, Collins suggests, we can decide where to go and how to get there.

Collins offers some valuable insights based on many years of research and observation. First recognize that change happens slowly. I can add from my own political experience that great change happens incrementally. Moving from a state of rest (inaction) to one of action requires a great deal of effort to start the motion. Collins likens the effort to a flywheel. Once the motion begins, it feeds on its own momentum and builds speed and power creating the "flywheel effect" which turns great effort into momentum in favor of the original source of the effort or energy.

The development of influential organizations requires a rather simplistic approach. First, get the right people, with valuable capacities. Second, have disciplined thought, keep things simple and focused, and know your skills, capability and capacity. Third, disciplined action and the "stop doing list" which requires a solid to do list and a solid list of things to stop because these activities add nothing to where you are going. If it doesn't directly achieve needed results, stop doing it.

How citizens' pressure groups destroy themselves

The first thing that must be recognized in any attempt to establish political pressure is that for the most part, these activities are initiated and conducted by volunteers.

This is a largely overlooked cause of low levels of citizen involvement in the politics of change. It is just easier for the average citizen to leave it alone. Even if a citizen is initially motivated to become active, those who organize such efforts need to understand the internal dynamics of all-volunteer groups.

Lack of attention to what can go wrong inside a group means countless grassroots initiatives wither and die without achieving anything. The problem is quite simply that many citizens groups drive away their most able members. In a typical arc, a new member will step forth to work with others on some public issue, last for a relatively short time, then disappear back into private life, never to be heard from again.

"The Citizen's Library" and "Community Organizing" sections of the Citizen's Handbook (Charles Dobson); and the community problem solving practices developed by the US National Civic League published in its journal The National Civic Review offers some of the following insights.

Too little fun

Long-term activists have fun when they get together. Many enjoy making fun of people in power. People who take themselves too seriously can turn any task into a chore. Getting together should feel more like recreation than work, no matter how serious the issue. Those who understand citizen involvement stress the importance of having fun over all other considerations. Politics is a social event. Leaders of these efforts need to find opportunities that allow people to be social, share ideas and opportunities to relax in and as part of the group. These create bonding opportunities. Bonding will create an esprit de corps that creates a dynamic that is powerful in motivating the group to press on.

Only an inner focus

When a citizens group becomes too focused on organization and too little focus on mission; it has a tendency to get bogged down. Hoping to become more organized, many small groups create little bureaucracies that drain everyone's energy. Often so much effort goes into maintaining the organization there is little left to pursue the reason for creating an organization in the first place. Beware of boards, forming a non-profit society, writing grant applications, fundraising, annual reports, Roberts Rules of Order and the other components of organizational quicksand. Personally I believe it robs the group of creativity and spontaneity.

A sign of trouble for citizens groups is a tendency for too many meetings and too little action. Most people would prefer to act on something concrete rather than sit at a meeting wrangling or trying to "reach consensus". Some meetings are usually necessary, but try to keep the frequency down, the time short and the number of participants small.

Other issues can be seen in too much deciding and too little creating. Every advocacy group needs to generate options for action. To do this well, participants need to switch off their Voice of Judgment and brainstorm. Unfortunately, when people get together for a meeting they usually switch on their Voice of Judgment in preparation for decision making. If they remain in this critical frame of mind, they will generate few options for action. Nothing will get done. No one will have any fun. Your cause will stall.

Too many people

Because of the emphasis on getting more people involved, many people feel that large groups are better than small groups. This is a mistake. A working group that plans directs and coordinates strategy and tactical implementation should not exceed nine people. This is not to imply that a large active group of volunteers is not desired or needed but from a leadership and planning perspective a smaller "inner circle" is needed. Nine persons is the upper limit of what sociologists call a primary group. A small group does not preclude working with others under the umbrella of a larger group; nor does it prelude communicating with larger numbers of people through email networks, special events and annual conventions.

The wrong people

As an extension of what Jim Collins has suggested in his book, "Good to Great", building democracy and community involves working with others. Most people assume they should welcome anyone interested in joining. But, this wholesome impulse can lead to rapid decline. Few are willing to admit what is obvious in any grassroots group. Some people are assets and others are liabilities. Every group can handle a small portion of people who are even angry, or combative, or controlling, or just lonely, or just out-to-lunch. As the ratio of these people increases, level-headed, friendly, competent people begin to leave.

As the imbalance increases, even more leave until the group is reduced to a grim residue. Those interested in growing the grassroots need to address this all too common phenomenon.

Too little contact

It is hard for people to maintain a working relationship when they see one another once a month. Once a week is best, not only because it is more frequent but because it fits into the way people schedule other activities. If regular face-to-face contact is difficult, regular phone calls or email may work as a substitute. More attention needs to be paid to unplanned getting together one of the traditional sources of community. Much of it used to occur on the street before cars took over. Today it occurs in the workplace, in places designed to enhance community. However; working with a close knit dedicated leadership core insures that the objectives do not out-match resources available for the group.

Groups of nine or less can often manage on personal resources. But as group size increases, a shortage of money and time usually leads to spiraling decline. Without paid staff there is no one to look after organizational housekeeping, and no one to train, manage and reward volunteers. As people disappear, many potential grassroots leaders burn out trying to do more and more themselves. A lack of resources does not mean giving up. It does mean inventing clever ways to effectively use time, connections and skills. In summary: limit group size to nine, make sure members enjoy one another's company, have fun, and avoid stretching resources.

Organize around Several Hot Issues

The ability to attract supporters and the ability to extend coalitions to various power groups is essential. People often organize around a single issue. They get together because they are annoyed or angry about street crime, taxes, or some zoning issue.

Often the issue is a proposed change or addition to the neighborhood that is seen as undesirable. Those in favor of changes or additions often describe this kind of activism as NIMBYism (Not-In-My-Back-Yard syndrome), a selfish attempt by residents to keep their part of town just as it is, in defiance of some larger public good. They rarely mention how the first towns arose out of the natural tendency for people to band together to oppose disruptive outside forces. A potential threat may be just what is needed to mobilize citizens.

Positive advocacy-Getting Heard

There are several possible obstacles to building a campaign for a proactive advocacy. The first and the most difficult obstacle is that of social inertia. People find it difficult to alter their lives because we are so busy with work, outside activities, taking kids to their overbook activities. While getting people to agree that a problem exist or a cause is worthy of support, they simply do not have the time or energy to become actively involved. If the community organizer can not motivate a core of key persons the probability of mounting any campaign that has the impact to cause politicians or bureaucrats to take notice and address the issue.

Another obstacle is that of financial resources. Some campaigns that need to promote public awareness and action, like corporate or political marketing campaigns will need dollars for the purchase of mailings and perhaps radio and TV media buys. In these cases, organizers will spend a great deal of their time in raising donations. This in and of itself can be a full time endeavor.

Building a Constituency

The ability to find an advocacy constituency is essential for building political clout. Without a visible constituency which has a demonstrated willingness and capacity to exert political pressure, little likelihood exists for causing change.

Building a constituency is a ground game requiring active interaction within the community. To win converts and support you must have the ability to factually support and defend your position and most importantly be able to express why the issue is important for those who you target for support.

Assuming that a citizen's group can build some critical mass, in order for it to be recognized as a potential threat or irritants to the targeted political leader it is a simple set of tactics that can be used to gain attention.

1. Generation of mass calls and letters is a time honored way to alert political forces that their political equilibrium is in jeopardy.
2. Demonstrations that garner media attention are also highly effective
3. Meeting with political leaders is probably the most effective method of getting heard.

Unfortunately, unless you are viewed as someone who can create political tension and jeopardy; meetings may not be easy to get from entrenched political leaders.

Finding Crusaders and Gladiators

The sometime Herculean effort to get citizens involved has perplexed the hardcore political activist for as long as we have engaged in the political process.

I thought that it may be of some interest to those reading this book in understanding the process of becoming a political activist and crusader. I believe such a look is helpful in recruiting and maintaining socio-political activist organizations.

How one Becomes a Political Crusader

When a citizen or a citizen's group decides to take-on the existing system to effect some sort of social change, they are in effect becoming crusaders for that change. Before becoming a crusader, most of those making that choice arrive at that decision through an evaluative process. Individuals that are in that process need to understand that becoming a crusader has a number of inherent risks associated with that decision. To some limited extent I have taken a look at the process of becoming a crusader or more specifically for this book, becoming a socio-political activist. Along with my own personal experience in this area, I have also taken a scholarly look at what others have learned from the examination of being a crusader. My examination has brought me to the research of Jai ping Wang, in her doctoral dissertation on the subject of Crusading (Wang 2006). While her study explored crusading for change in the workplace, many elements of her Theory of Crusading are appropriate in a socio-political context outside of the workplace.

The Decision to Become a Political Crusader or Gladiator

Assessing the political and personal environment includes evaluating the political climate and the feasibility for change along with the potential crusaders personal circumstances. In essence the potential political activist-crusader engages in a cost benefit feasibility assessment. The current political situation and history, present circumstances and some insight as to if the climate is suitable for making major changes become important elements of the personal assessment. Individual crusaders must evaluate these elements before and during their journey of socio-political activism.

Based on their personal assessment, individuals determine and adjust their priorities as well as their tactics. We will explore a variety of tactics available later in this effort. Individuals are also sensitive to their immediate environment that is often displayed in their community surroundings. For instance, individuals gauge who are key players, what are taboo issues within the current political environment, and what are respected customs within the immediate environment.

Typical political taboos could cover a wide range of issues and tied to social and political ideologies. Examples are found in political social ideologies tied to Gay rights, abortion and foreign involvement in political processes. This understanding is essential for anyone considering a social crusade. It serves as establishing the guidelines for avoiding unnecessarily stepping on too many toes, especially those they cannot afford to cross. Picking the wrong social convention to challenge within a group can quickly lead to being exposed to forces that eliminate your crusade as any threat to the status quo formulated as a result of a strict ideology. Knowing this in advance saves individuals from wasting time and effort on initiatives that are unlikely to yield desirable results.

Most important of all, that understanding helps individuals sustain their activism without sustaining fatal blows.

The evaluation of individuals' personal situations such as job security, career prospect, family and standing among peers and the social community plays a crucial role in determining one's primary involvement in political activism.

Frequently, changes in one aspect of the environment call for new assessment of one or more aspects of the total environment.

Changes in individuals' personal environment such as health and/or family require them to reassess and readjust their socio-political activism commitment. Organizational leadership change may affect individual's assessment of their organization, their judgment of organizational priorities and therefore, their objectives of social-political socio-political activism.

Assessing Environment and Purposes of Crusading

The outcome of the personal assessment has a direct impact on individuals' priorities in terms of choice of socio-political activism goals. When members of the socio-political environ-ment perceive that the status quo to be less than desirable, the drive to better their situation often overpowers other lesser needs and wants. In environments where members yearn for more unity, the initiatives that promote harmony are more likely to be endorsed. For individuals whose social-cultural security is still uncertain, their socio-political activism priori-ties are usually in alignment with their efforts in promoting both group harmony and change. This is generally a position of weakness and illustrative of a lack of personal power.

The accurate and timely assessment of the political envi-ronment is a prerequisite for adopting appropriate and effec-tive tactics throughout one's socio-political activism. The outcome of an environmental assessment guides individuals in selecting and adopting tactics that will not only enhance their effectiveness but also seek to protect individuals engaged in socio-political activism.

Due to the dynamic nature of political environments, assessment is generally conducted continuously. When indi-viduals realize the vulnerability of their position within a com-munity due to their low level of power or influence, they tend to adopt less aggressive tactics of political activism or they decide that the risk of involvement is personally greater than the risk of staying on the sidelines.

Between Fear and Hope

Individuals engaged in socio-political activism have the gen-eral nature of believing in hope. They also believe in preserving themselves while engaged in socio-political activism. Without preserving themselves, activism for hope will not be possible. Therefore, for most activists, keeping one's affiliation with their peers and community safe and secure is the priority. That sense of safety and security includes several areas; personal security, community status, and future prospects.As such;

political organizers need to be able show compelling evidence that by joining the "crusade" will not place ones personal and emotional self in jeopardy, but may in fact, enhance them.

Between Desire and Reality

Balancing between desire and reality is another challenge faced by community leaders in order to engage in an effective socio-political activism and the activity necessary to effect and to sustain change.

In other words, balancing desire with reality is necessary both for the ultimate success of activism effort as well as maintaining the spirit of citizen involvement. To effectively practice balancing between desire and reality, individuals have to know what is desired and what is feasible. What is desired frames one's objectives for socio-political activism. What is feasible captures the political and community climate and one's own surroundings for socio-political activism. Practicing balancing between desire and reality provides both rationale and strategy for realistic and effective political action.

Balancing between Efforts and Results

Once individuals are involved in the socio-political activism process, they expect their effort to pay off with results. The balance between efforts and results are, therefore, crucial for individuals to sustain their enthusiasm and efforts. Lack of results can cause individuals to feel that their time, energy, experience, and expertise are wasted. It can also contribute to a feeling that they are not successful in making a difference, which is a crucial part of socio-political activism.

The balance between efforts and results is, therefore, also a validating process. Being able to witness results of their socio-political activism efforts allow individuals to develop a sense of pride for having made a difference. Not being able to produce results makes individuals feel a sense of resentment, and sometimes even anger. They are resentful both at themselves for making such a poor judgment by investing their time, energy, experience, and expertise in some fruitless exercises. They resent those who are responsible for not allowing their efforts to be productive and fruitful. In the mind of those engaged in socio-political activism, being able to produce results is a validation of their value and contribution to socio-political activism.

Efforts

Individuals' efforts are their contribution of time, energy, experience, expertise and sometimes money. Individuals' direct involvement or by supporting those who are directly involved. Direct contribution of time and energy is essential. Individuals devote time and energy for the designated cause for which they are socio-political activism. They utilize their experience and expertise to maximize their time and energy commitment toward positive outcomes. Individuals' experience and expertise enable them to crusade smartly. Indirect efforts involve supporting those who are directly engaged in socio-political activism both morally and literally by lending a hand.

Individuals provide indirect support for socio-political activism for a number of reasons. First, individuals may not be able to participate physically, but they believe in the cause. Therefore, they lend their ideological, moral, or financial support. Second, individuals may yield the front stage role to those whom they deem more appropriate while they take a back-stage role in a particular socio-political activism effort. Last but not least, individuals may not feel comfortable enough to be directly involved in a socio-political activism effort for fear of personal security, community status, or future prospects. They delegate their desire and wish to those who do not have that discomfort and quietly support those who are championing on the stage. This is delegating to "gladiators". Regardless of the form of efforts and the format in which efforts are made, individuals expect results from their socio-political activism efforts and they make their best attempts to maximize results for their efforts.

Results

The results individuals expect come in two categories: tangible and intangible. Tangible results include one or more of the following: outcomes, recognition, and respect. Intangible results can be increased awareness and sensitivity. In the area of tangible results, most frequently individuals expect concrete outcomes for their socio-political activism efforts such as a new policy, a new procedure, or an improved community conditions. Other times when immediate concrete results are not possible or visible, less tangible results such as recognition and respect from peers and community can fill in the void. Tangible results coupled with duly received recognition and respect make individuals feel accomplished in their journey of socio-political activism, which is, in turn, a great incentive for further socio-political activism efforts.

★ ★ **CHAPTER** ★ ★

13

Putting Community Forces
in Action

Chapter 13

Putting Community Forces in Action

Vision without implementation is merely a hallucination.
– *Albert Einstein*

In the earlier case study, residents in Hill Top and Lake Side found strength and common purpose in the discussion surrounding the decay of the community. These communities had dormant neighborhood organizations until the communities saw a rise in crime, a drop in real estate sales and depressed housing prices. As a result of defending against political non-decisions, these communities suddenly found the need for a neighborhood voice over proposed zoning changes that threatened the value of older houses and the rise of low-cost rental accommodations. Sometimes an issue can serve to invigorate an existing organization.

Organizing around a hot issue can be a waste of time if it leads to a hardening of positions. Too often, citizens have worn themselves out in fights between themselves. This has allowed the political leadership to sit back and avoid the personal threat to their power which the group may have provided if not for the infighting over other issues. Community organizing and action needs to take a battlefield approach, building strength, or the appearance of strength, that threatens political stability. It is the only way to influence public decision-making.

Getting Noticed

Getting positive political results often means engaging in activities that draws attention to your issue or cause. Often the value of shedding light on a politician's actions or inactions is immeasurable. Remember that the political image is perhaps the most valuable assets a politician has and any potential for image damage or enhancement is a tool that citizens groups can and should utilize.

In addition, if you need more mass support and active involved workers, you will probably want to expand the number of people who know what you are doing. The bottom line is you need to get noticed. In today's environment, this usually means working with the media. Publicity has the added power of buoying up participants, bringing in more volunteers, nudging bureaucrats, unhinging politicians, and adding momentum to a grassroots initiative. Also, proving that you as an individual or as a group can access media immediately gives your issue and group legitimacy. Such legitimacy demands action.

Empowerment comes from simple exposure. "Group members say, 'Did you see we were in the news again. Isn't it great? We are really starting to get places now.'"

When you have an understanding of the media and what issues or actions attract their attention, you can raise public issues that are being ignored and reframe issues from a citizen's perspective. A word of caution here, be very careful and suspicious of reporters. In most cases they are not there to be your advocates. Many, if not most, journalists look for stories rooted in conflict, error, and injustice. They may impose a confrontational agenda that can actually make it more difficult for you to resolve your issue. Always, always, speak respectfully of opponents. Do not inflame their base supporters unless you are willing and fully equipped for war.

As preparation for gaining notice, particularly media attention the steps should be taken as suggested in "The Citizen's Handbook" (Dobson):

1. Assemble a list of sympathetic journalists.
2. Find the media professionals in your community
3. Define your messages, and then create your quotes.
4. Make actions newsworthy.
5. Look for timing opportunities.
6. Write letters to the editor
7. Issue media advisories
8. Aim at Television
9. Practice your blurb
10. Don't rely on the media to educate
11. Use all the other media

A Process Model for Shifting Public Opinion

Shifting public opinion, and therefore getting politicians to change their position, is tied to a unique set of actions designed to steer the course of public opinion.

First, Shifting behaviors or tactics is an ideological exercise with the purpose of drawing others into the debate. Once engaged in the debate, your cause and position immediately becomes both legitimate and newsworthy. This legitimacy is essential in building a power base. Only through this activity can citizens groups muster enough influence to cause large numbers of persons to be swayed or "shifted" in their opinions and support for the opposition.

The shifting process has distinct stages. I identify them as;

a. Issuing
b. Vetting/testing
c. Strategy Design
d. Coalition building
e. Repositioning

Issuing Stage

This stage begins when community activists brainstorm to articulate the critical issues that will be used to gain a broad base of political support. This requires a measure of testing relevance of issues for the broader community. This process has three properties, they include "seeking" activities, "pleading" activities and "consensus building" activities. If you feel you have read these previously in this book you have. These are remarkably similar to actions taken by political leaders and politicians in building their power base. If you are engaged in this process, you are now engaged in the Hardball actions of the political process.

"Seeking" actions, are those activities that will allow you to find followers. That means becoming visible and vocal. The pleading action is asking for support in the form of others speaking out, financial support, or even backroom operations support.

"Consensus" building is the attempt to build a critical mass or the allusion of a critical mass of support. This effort is essential in building the power to shift a political position.

Vetting/Testing stage

This stage is the process of developing your argument and evaluating the strength of your argument along with the ability to raise support. At this point, community activist will have to identify the elements or factors that have any cause and effect impacts. In essence you seek to identify factors that could derail or neutralize your efforts. In general, you are becoming "environmentally aware" of your playing field. There is nothing like an unexpected blindsiding to render you a non-factor in forcing debate or change.

Once the issues and a position on the issues are defined, it is time to test their validity with peers and other opinion leaders. This is an opportunity to fine tune any area that does not or has not articulated well. This step of trial by peer has a tendency to battle harden the effort. This effort allows for other opinion leaders an opportunity to subjectively evaluate your proposed action and most importantly the proposed new policy versus the merits of the existing policy. Without the ability to sell the merits of the new approach, you will be unable to neither build support nor influence public officials to act. Failure to prove the merit can also be viewed as an opportunity for more input and perhaps a reformulation of the proposed change.

Strategy Design Stage

This stage is one of selection. Does the situation demand a show of force in terms of public confrontation or does a non-public show of power to the politician of bureaucrat make sense? Do you use threat in order to derail, create political disequilibrium, or does it make sense to enter the scene as a potential ally and supporter? My own preference is to always engage the power of niceness. Seek to become an ally first with the implied threat that you have options.

Coalition Building Stage

This is an essential step in building any level of power and influence. The ability to cause a shift in public opinion or a shift in the position of an obstructionist politico has been used as the theme for this book. Action is based on the citizens ability to create some sort of political disequilibrium. Much if not all of the ability to create political stress is based on the ability to form coalitions between enough community groups to form a true power base. Even diverse groups with seemingly little in common, can be brought together for a common cause or a cause that in some way benefits any of the parties. Hopefully this group was pulled together during earlier stages.

The critical component actions needed to bring groups together is first and foremost a method of communication. This can be in the form of group meeting; Web based community building programs, newsletters or old fashioned telephone banks and door to door campaigns. Through the use of the various communication methods, a message that seeks to reinforce the need for the proposed community action must be the centerpiece of any communication. Communication needs to also be directed at the public policy makers which is the step of putting them on notice that action is happening. The public at large should also be communicated with through news outlets in hopes of garnering additional support. This is exactly how one of our study communities was able to have the ACLU and the NAACP to enter the community action program.

When Confrontation is required

In some cases, all the good planning and attempts to create a state of political disequilibrium in a forceful direct way is simply rebuffed. Perhaps the developed coalitions are perceived as weak of not strongly committed. In this situation it may be appropriate to do battle in a more aggressive mode. The "in your face" approach can be effective but it is an escalation that gets down, dirty and personal. It is not an approach for the faint of heart. Much of this approach was developed during the 1960's.

Something can be learned from the tactics used by the radicals of the 60's. My whole approach in getting what you want politically is tied to the ability to either create extreme and very public disequilibrium or at bringing ridicule and public embarrassment.

The radicals of the 60's used a continuous and unrelenting pressure that brought down the presidency of Lyndon Johnson over the Viet Nam war in 1968. Some of the collective process can be examined in terms of strategy and tactical applications.

In 1971, Saul Alinsky wrote an entertaining classic on grassroots organizing titled "Rules for Radicals". Much of what he observed and developed was learned by his involvement in the anti-war effort that brought down the administration of Lyndon Johnson. President Johnson was in reality driven from office by this political movement.

In the current politically correct environment, that insists on cooperative and civil social problem solving, most current activists would denounced such approaches. Nevertheless, Alinsky provides some of the best advice on confrontational tactics. As he points out, radical approaches are for those who as "have nots" are seeking ways to take it away from the perceived to "**have it alls**".

Alinski practiced what he preached. He said... "Tactics means doing what you can with what you have... tactics is the art of how to take and how to give." He uses eyes, ears and nose for examples.

"Eyes -"If you have a vast organization, parade it before the enemy, openly show your power."

"Ears - "If your organization is small, do what Gideon did: conceal the members in the dark but raise a clamor that will make the listener believe that your organization numbers many more that it does."

"Nose -"If your organization is too tiny even for noise, stink up the place."

These tactics go a great way to threaten the disequilibrium that political leaders will move mountains to avoid. Alinski devised and proved thirteen tactical rules for use against opponents vastly superior in power and wealth. To paraphrase some sage advice, "keep your friends close, keep your enemies closer." If your business or organization ever becomes a target of radical activists, it will be extremely helpful to know what strategies of attack will be used against you. Short of having spies infiltrate their organization - a practice that is sure to be found out and exposed to your discredit - it would help to study their methods.

The ability of grassroots groups to apply pressure on large social and that the ability will continue. Because political conflicts occur in high-profile public view, an often-panicked political decision-maker, will often help organizations develop counteractive strategies that can level the playing field and deflect the effort to Shore-up.

Governments and social organizations have inherent weaknesses. Time and again, they repeat mistakes that other large organizations have made, even repeating their OWN mistakes.

Political leaders have learned to stonewall and not empower activists. They try to ignore radical activists. It often seems as if politicians are never as willing to pay the price for victory, as their opposition is in total commitment to defeating them. Politicians that lose elements of their power base are unprepared for the hailstorm of brutal tactics that severely damage their reputation and send them running from public office.

Some of these tactics are ruthless, but they work. Here are the Alinski's rules that the political activist can utilize to get and keep political opposition off balance;

Tactic 1: *"Power is not only what you have, but what the enemy thinks you have." Power is derived from 2 main sources - money and people. "Have-Nots" must build power from flesh and blood. (These are two things of which there is a plentiful supply. Government and corporations always have a difficult time appealing to people, and usually do so almost exclusively with economic arguments.)*

Tactic 2: *"Never go outside the expertise of your people." It results in confusion, fear and retreat. Feeling secure adds to the backbone of anyone. (Organizations under attack wonder why radicals don't* *address the "real" issues. This is why. They avoid things with which they have no knowledge.)*

Tactic 3: *"Whenever possible, go outside the expertise of the enemy." Look for ways to increase insecurity, anxiety and uncertainty. (This happens all the time. Watch how many organizations under attack are blind-sided by seemingly irrelevant arguments that they are then forced to address.)*

Tactic 4: *"Make the enemy live up to its own book of rules." If the rule is that every letter gets a reply, send 30,000 letters. You can kill them with this because no one can possibly obey all of their own rules. (This is a serious rule. The besieged entity's very credibility and reputation is at stake, because if activists catch it lying or not living up to its commitments, they can continue to chip away at the damage.)*

Tactic 5: *"Ridicule is man's most potent weapon." There is no defense. It's irrational. It's infuriating. It also works as a key pressure point to force the enemy into concessions.*

Tactic 6: *"A good tactic is one your people enjoy." They'll keep doing it without urging and come back to do more. They're doing their thing, and will even suggest better ones. (Radical activists, in this sense, are no different that any other human being. We all avoid "un-fun" activities, and but we revel at and enjoy the ones that work and bring results.)*

Tactic 7: *"A tactic that drags on too long becomes a drag." Don't become old news. (Even radical activists get bored. So to keep them excited and involved, organizers are constantly coming up with new tactics.)*

Tactic 8: *"Keep the pressure on. Never let up." Keep trying new things to keep the opposition off balance. As the opposition masters one approach, hit them from the flank with something new. (Attack, attack, attack from all sides, never giving the reeling organization a chance to rest, regroup, recover and re-strategize.)*

Tactic 9: *"The threat is usually more terrifying than the thing itself." Imagination and ego can dream up many more consequences than any activist. (Perception is reality. Large organizations always* *prepare a worst-case scenario, something that may be furthest from the activists' minds. The upshot is that the organization will expend enormous time and energy, creating in its own collective mind the direst of conclusions. The possibilities can easily poison the mind and result in demoralization.)*

Tactic 10: *"If you push a negative hard enough, it will push through and become a positive." Violence from the other side can win the public to your side because the public sympathizes with the underdog. (Unions used this tactic. Peaceful [albeit loud] demonstrations during the heyday of unions in the early to mid-20th Century incurred management's wrath, often in the form of violence that eventually brought public sympathy to their side.)*

Tactic 11: *"The price of a successful attack is a constructive alternative." Never let the enemy score points because you're caught without a solution to the problem. (Old saw: If you're not part of the solution, you're part of the problem. Activist organizations have an agenda, and their strategy is to hold a place at the table, to be given a forum to wield their power. So, they have to have a compromise solution.)*

Tactic 12: *Pick the target, freeze it, personalize it, and polarize it." Cut off the support network and isolate the target from sympathy. Go after people and not institutions; people hurt faster than institutions. (This is cruel, but very effective. Direct, personalized criticism and ridicule works.)"*

The real action is in the enemy's reaction. The enemy properly goaded and guided in his reaction will be your major strength.

Tactics, like life, require that you move with the action."
"Alinski was hated and defamed by powerful enemies, proof that his tactics worked. His simple formula for success is useful to examine here...

"Agitate + Antagonize + Educate + Organize".

Here's how

Radical activism is characterized most by what it leaves aside. That is analysis and rhetorical positioning. It is neither about political, social or moral beliefs, bearing witness, nor convincing anyone of the rightness of anything. Rather, it deals with uniting people so they may strike at the causes of their concerns by utilizing power as they see fit.

Radical activists who work for meaningful change know that all effective organizing is local. They've learned the battles will be about small goals which immediately affect those involved. They strive for neighborhood control of a school program in order that their children are better educated. They protest to shut down a bank with discriminatory lending practices. They sit in an office in order to bring a campus to a halt because their teacher was unjustly fired. They picket and organize boycotts to decrease profit of a business harming their community. They jam and disrupt a government meeting to prevent passage of an injurious law. In sum, they apply power as necessary to gain, preserve, or take back what they believe is inherently theirs.

People did not suffer blows marching over the Edmund Pettus Bridge in order to cause passage of a national right to vote law. They did it to bring normal operation of the small town of Selma, Alabama to a stand still and force it to register black people to vote. To exactly the same ends but geographically removed, 1000 participants in the Mississippi Freedom Democratic Party filled the jails of Jackson, Mississippi. They succeeded because local garbage collection was stopped and the city budget drained. The trucks had to be used instead for hauling demonstrators who then had to be fed with funds otherwise available for normal operation.

The social changes that activist desire takes place when enough activists bring a halt to enough sectors of society which are then no longer able to continue operation in their previous modes. The changes occur because of the establishment's attempt to maintain power by mollifying and co-opting the impetus for continued collective activism. In trying to halt the activism, the establishment is itself changed. And, the liberals, who, analyzed, postulated, and talked but did little; gather credit for the emergence of their ideas. That they do is of little concern to the activists, who go on to organize further.

As offered by Saul Alinski; "Anyone can be a radical activist. It is easy. There is no need for profound social or political insight and analysis. Such is not only not required, but discouraged, for it only gets in the way. Following the simple steps will allow anyone to start a local movement. I have personally used them to initiate formation of effective civil rights, anti-war, and antipoverty groups. The technique worked every time."

The following was offered as an approach from a political campaign worker. He volunteered that it was not original but he did not know its origin. It appears to be somewhat similar to things previously offered by Alinski;

1. *Identify about six persons who do not particularly know each other but share somewhat similar views to your own. This is similar to my earlier coalition building but this time on a much smaller scale. This small group can create considerable "buzz" through such efforts as letters to the editor, start water cooler and/or after church discussions, make vocal statements in a social setting, club, or bar, and seek out like minded persons. Discuss positions, passions but don't discuss tactics, strategies, or solutions. Don't preach. Listen. Focus on those with intense feelings but avoid know-it-alls. Try to pick persons of divergent community status in so far as possible. Note how to contact them.*

2. *Meet separately, privately, and one time only with each of those you've identified. Invite them to your home or visit theirs. Go out to lunch or for drinks together. This time discuss your concerns in depth. Most importantly, listen to their views. Don't bring up organizing for action.*

3. *Arrange a meeting with the entire group together. Shut up. Let them talk. You will hear your own views presented to you as*

theirs. Agree with and reinforce those ideas, but don't expand them. Let them enjoy the shared feelings among new found friends. Keep things going until someone besides you suggest and the group agrees to meet again. Someone will, and they will. Have a place and time ready.

4. *At the next meeting encourage the group to initiate some kind of visible public action that will attract more participants. It should be fun and not too risky. Don't try to lead but just be one of the new movements. Enjoy!*

As the group enlarges and engages in actions, it will take directions depending on the inclinations and experience of the members. Be one of them. If they don't go your way, or even if they do, go start another. Then bring them together. Repeat. That's what radical organizing and therefore real democracy is all about.

The approach is for those who want to change the world from what it is to what they believe it should be.

The Prince was written by Machiavelli for the Haves on how to hold power which has been modernized and explained in the previous section with my theory of Shoring-Up as a political process. According to Alinsky, the main job of the organizer is to bait an opponent into reacting. "The enemy properly goaded and guided in his reaction will be your major strength."

Use this growing band of "concerned citizens' to be present at public events when public officials are present. Become visible and vocal. Call out politicians to debate whenever the opportunity is present. Demand meeting to discuss the issue in public forums. The politician or bureaucrat loses if he rebuffs you and he loses if he offers a meeting. Invite the media or press to any meeting. Even if they don't take the bait, you are creating at the least discomfort and the illusion of strength with the ability to create a political imbalance (Disequilibrium)

CHAPTER

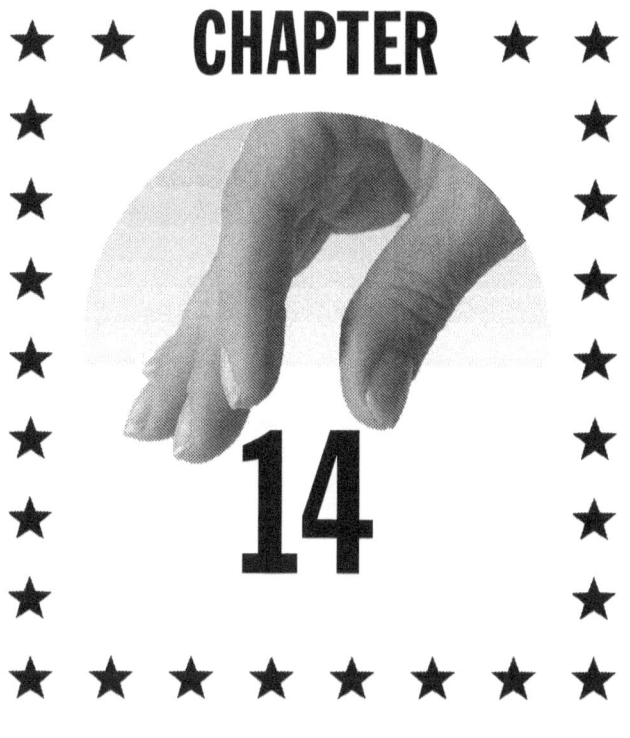

14

So What?

Chapter 14

So What?

Politics is messy, it's unpredictable. Some political scientists have referred to it as chaotic and the ultimate maze (Stone, 2002). Yet it is through this chaos that civilization functions, grows and even survives by way of the political process. To understand the causes and types of behavior that political players and society engage is to understand ourselves and society.

Political decision making is interesting in a number of ways but particularly interesting that in some vague way the general populace views the process as corrupt and even dirty. Stone (2002. p.376) even suggests that Americans would rather replace the entire process with rational decision making. The theory of Shoring-Up demonstrates that political decision making is rational. It is rational in a way that society forces an approach to political decision making that demands immediate action and generally forces the taking of sides.

The rational model of decision making is forged through the process of reasoning by calculation. Political leadership and the holding of power are dependent upon the politician's ability to calculate consequences and to count heads with every society forced decision. As the rational model demands, there are facts underlying all situations and political decisions. Politics may be energized by emotion but its decisions are cold hard calculation weighing the consequences as a threat to power.

Political reasoning and decisions are always conducted as part of that struggle. Politics and the political process is the ultimate reality show. The stakes are high, there are winners and losers. Political process is designed to control the immediate making long term solutions very difficult. Shoring-Up behavior is a political behavior geared for political survival.

The survival instinct in a politician is an important attribute if they are to be successful as apolitical leader. Political reason and decision making is a process of persuasion. It is a process of winning the hearts and minds of the populace so that some greater vision can be pursued.

The savvy community leader can achieve the desired political favors and interventions by adjusting approaches towards political leaders. In creating an environment or an approach that limits threats to the political equilibrium, community leader lessen or eliminate the propensity of politicians to seek and engage in Shoring-Up behaviors.

Community leaders need to adopt a philosophy of limiting tension creating behaviors that lead to a disequilibrium or derailment of the political leader's vision but instead look for common ground upon which to agree. Differing interpretation tend to divide people. Seeking to define and combine aspirations will usually unite a community.

Understanding the Shoring-Up behavior and its processes can help both politicians and community leaders understand the nature of the political realities and can offer insights into the creation of methods and procedures for seeking and obtaining final solutions to the constant and universal problems that plague our communities.

The theory of Shoring-up is an articulation and integration of observations, ideas, behaviors strategies and tactical applications that have emerged from the core variable and concisely demonstrates how political leaders when confronted with challenges to their status or power begin a set of behaviors that follows a precise pattern that is calculated, formalized and prescriptive for the sole purpose of eliminating or marginalizing opponents that pose any threat.

The theory is significant in that it for the first time identifies behaviors and patterns in political executive decision processes that lies somewhere in between popular concepts of "Satisficing behaviors" (Simon, 1957),and those attributed to the variety of approaches to strategic decision making. This "new space" has yet to this point in time enumerated in the management or political science literature.

Shoring-up behaviors operate in a sequential and recursive pattern of threat identification leading to the strategies and tactics to render such threats harmless. Interview data would suggest that Shoring-up is at times both a conscious and unconscious reflexive response by political leaders.

As illuminated in chapter four, the basis for Shoring-up behaviors is rooted in the core beliefs and the espoused visions of those who seek and or hold political office. The theory identifies this process as Forging. It is Forging that melds these sets of beliefs and vision that shoring-up behaviors are directed toward protecting.

The seeking and the retention of political power and elected office often hinges on the ability of the politician and those around him to sense threats to the political powerbase or to the programs and tactics that assist movement towards the vision. The Sensing stage of the theory identifies the conditions of tension, political disequilibrium and threats of derailment to the vision. The sensing stage is where political disruptions are at a level to become noticed. A shift or unexpected change in this level can lead to conditions that insure Shoring-up behaviors given that the threat is assessed as dangerous. The theory identifies the next sequential stage as that of Reacting to the changes in the political environment that offer the potential for a threat to the vision and political power.

The actions found in reacting are scanning, assessing, and diffusing. Each of these actions has a distinct function. Scanning is the process of monitoring the political environment this is done on a constant basis. Typical scans include monitoring the economic, social-cultural, legal and regulatory environments for indications that any change may have either a positive or negative impact on the reaching of the vision. This is a more targeted and purposeful look at the environment versus what the theory identifies in the Sensing stage. The difference lies in that scanning is a deliberate and organized activity whereas; sensing is triggered by a perceptual change by the politician in the environment caused by deliberate actions or reaction from opposition groups.

The Assessing activity is more or less the evaluation of the information derived from the Scanning process. The assessment will allow the political leader to select one of three strategies to address information from the scan. The strategies are to engage in overt offensive mode behaviors to address an either positive or negative issue or take on a defensive mode to protect an attack from the opposition or decide that no action is necessary. The choice of strategy will be tied to what is believed to be necessary to maintain the political equilibrium. If an action is required to re-establish equilibrium, the theory states that the process of Shoring-up moves to the action strategy of Diffusing. The object of Diffusing is to first lower or eliminate the built up political tension. Once tension has been lessened, the strategy move to find methods that will restore a state of equilibrium and make the initial attempts to return to the vision.

Once the strategies and tactics are deployed to re-establish political control and to diffuse any power that the opposition forces had mustered, it is vital that the political leaders quickly to an environment that is as close as possible to the original state. This stage of the theory has been identified as the Normalizing stage. It is in this stage as the theory states that all players from both the opposition and the internal support groups must be brought to their original positions of acceptance. This is accomplished through the use of justifying strategies as stated in detail in chapter four. Additionally, the politician must work at reinforcing his support through the use of rewards and punishment for supporter and any who tried to oppose the mission and vision. The politician will then move to consolidate power and if possible find support from the ranks of the defeated in order to solidify and expand the support base.

This is the political process of Shoring-up. For the political player, it is a natural way of life. It is easily observable. It tends to be a process that is not turned on and off as needed but a continuous and recursive process.

Reflections

The model of Shoring-up offers an insight into the political decision making process that is perhaps unique in that the data for the theory was derived for the most part, from the political players themselves. Through observations, interviews and experience, the emergence of the theory of Shoring–up establishes reasonable analysis and explanation of certain political behavior and decision making processes.

It is also important to note that political leadership may in fact be a study in followership in that successful political leaders must acquire the skills and mindset to be a follower of the power constituencies that vote and keep them in office. While some would perhaps seek to eliminate the Shoring-up behaviors because it seems to be counter productive to solving basic social issues and problems; it is possible that attempts to thwart Shoring-Up behavior will not work because the political system is designed in such a way that the political leader can only respond with Shoring-Up behaviors for fear of alienating any support base.

In this circumstance, it is better to recognize and understand the behavior in order to recognize the reality of situations and to perhaps engage in constituent behaviors that forces the appropriate political response to the problem for which redress is sought.

A key finding in the theory research is recognizing that Shoring-Up is a political leader's resistance to taking definitive action towards a final solution for fear of losing power and position. My experience and observations tell me that any political initiative on the part of the political leader that is a diversion or a delay to making an absolute decision is usually an indication that disequilibrium is expected or feared.

Our recent models of political leadership all depend on fairly high levels of generalized deference; while there are general institutional constraints on what a president can do, the public's orientation has been to give the people it elects a great deal of leeway to choose a particular set of foreign and domestic policies. Unless these policies produce disaster in the form of significant American casualties or highly visible domestic economic difficulties, approval ratings tend to remain quite high. This is precisely the context in which image management and public relations become more central to the exercise of presidential power than policy initiatives. (Block, 1989, p. 228)

The reality of the situation at this point is that community leaders have two choices. The first is to seek accommodation and attempt to relieve tension and potential disequilibrium. The second is to prepare for confrontation and the creation of opposition groups to either change the will of the political leader and their supporters or in a democratic society seek to remove or replace a leader that can not maintain the majority support.

The savvy community leader can achieve the desired political favors and interventions by adjusting approaches towards political leaders. Political leaders will respond to opportunities to expand support groups much easier than they will react to a perceived threat or confrontation. In creating an environment or an approach that limits threats to the political equilibrium, community leader lessen or eliminate the propensity of politicians to seek and engage in Shoring-up behaviors.

Community leaders need to adopt a philosophy of limiting tension creating behaviors that lead to a disequilibrium or derailment of the political leader's vision but instead look for common ground upon which to agree. Differing interpretation tend to divide people. Seeking to define and combine aspirations will usually unite a community.

Understanding the Shoring-Up behavior and its processes can help both politicians and community leaders understand the nature of the political realities and can offer insights into the creation of methods and procedures for seeking and obtaining final solutions to the constant and universal problems that plague our communities

The long-term effect of Shoring-Up behavior is that because of political expediency, the real causes of social problems and conflict can never directly be addressed. The use of Shoring-up behaviors puts into play other forces that have an impact on the community. Since the local community is a working system, any change in the inputs or changes in the processing elements that make the system work will have effects on the workings of the community system. The adjustment of any input could change the dynamics of the system. At its core, Shoring-up behavior in the long run is the conscious effort to push difficult or politically unattractive decisions off until some time in the future while still diffusing high tension situations and maintaining a political equilibrium.

The politician thusly skillfully avoids the political fallout associated with politically incorrect or sensitive solutions and in some cases can push the decision off to another political office holder in the future. However, the use of short-term Shoring-up activity can affect the political and social relationships within the community system.

The Shoring-up approach is designed to address only the symptomatic consequences of some underlying cause to the extent that political pressure is reduced. The use of Shoring-up interventions adversely affects the possibility of a final solution in that the pressure within the social system is lessened to the point that short-term equilibrium is established. This state, in-turn, eliminates the need to find the ultimate solution now even when it is evident that the problem will return in the future. The need to "fix" social security so that it remains a viable and solvent program is a prime example of this state. It is the prime example of the power of a small group of power holders. It exemplifies the art of the non-decision while simulating that actions are being considered, commissions staffed, investigations in force all seeking to solve this social dilemma. America, it is time we take our system back!

BONUS

Community Wellness
Assessment Worksheet

Plus

Your 10 steps for Community Action
A Value of up to $1,500.00 !!

The goal of these worksheets is to help you establish a clear understanding of whether your community leaders are doing the job. Once you have taken and graded your community wellness audit you will clearly see if your community is at risk and the steps you and your community member can take to reclaim control of the political process to repair at risk communities.

By completing the worksheet, you will maximize your potential benefits gained from reading and using the processes presented in *"The Strategic Citizen"*

An onsite evaluation by the Dr. Patnode using the assessment tool exceeds $1,500

They are available to you at www.strategiccitizen.com

BIBLIOGRAPHY

Arnold, R. Douglas (1990). The Logic of Congressional Action New Haven, CT: Yale University Press.

Bass, Bernard M. (1981). Stogdill's Handbook of Leadership. New York: Free Press.

Bennis, W. (1993). "An Invented Life: Reflections on Leadership and Change", Addison-Wesley Publishing Company, reprinted from the summer 1994 issue of USC Business.

Blake, Robert & Mouton, Jane (1984). The Managerial Grid. Houston, TX: Golf Publication.

Block, F. (1989). 11. Modernity, Democracy, and the Problem of Authority*. In Social Class and Democratic Leadership: Essays in Honor of E. Digby Baltzell, Bershady, H. J. (Ed.) (pp. 216-28). Philadelphia: University of Pennsylvania Press.

Bolman, L. G. & Deal, T. E. (1991). Reframing Organizations: Artistry, choice and leadership. San Francisco: Jossey-Bass.

Bonner, H. (1959). Group Dynamics Principles and Applications. New York: Ronald Press Co.

Brown, J. F. (1936). Psychology and the Social Order: An Introductions to the Dynamic Study of Social Fields (1st ed.). New York: Mc-Graw-Hill Book Company, Inc.

Burns, James, M. (1978). "Leadership". New York: Harper Row.

Burnstein, Paul (2003) "The Impact of Public Opinion on Public Policy". Political Research Quarterly. (Vol. 56, pp. 29-40).

Caddy, Douglas. 1974. The Hundred Million Dollar Payoff. Arlington House: New Rochelle, NY.

Chenitz, W. C., & Swanson, J. M. (1986). From practice to grounded theory. Menlo Park, CA: Addison-Wesley Publishing Company.

De Grazia, Alfred, Political Behavior (2004). Retrieved from www. Grazian-archives.com/politics/political behavior/C-o1.html.on 2/23/2004

Dobson, Charles. (2005) The Citizen's Handbook / Vancouver Citizen's Committee

Domhoff, G. William (1998). Who Rules America: Power and Politics in the year 2000? Mountain View, CA: Mayfield

Dye, Thomas R. (2002). Understanding Public Policy. 10th ed. Upper Saddle River, NJ: Prentice Hall.

Fiedler, F. E. & Chemers, M. M. (1974). Leadership and effective management. New York: Scott-Foresman.

Gardner, John (1990). On Leadership. New York: The Free Press.

Glaser, B. G., Ph.D. (1965). The constant comparative method of qualitative analysis. Social Problems, (pp. 12, 436-45).

Glaser, B. G., Ph.D., & Strauss, A. L., Ph.D. (1967). The discovery of grounded theory. Mill Valley, CA: Sociology Press.

Glaser, B. G., Ph.D. (1978). Advances in the methodology of grounded theory: Theoretical sensitivity. Mill Valley, CA: Sociology Press.

Glaser, B. G., Ph.D. (1992). Basics of grounded theory analysis: Emergence versus forcing. Mill Valley, CA: Sociology Press.

Glaser, B. G., Ph.D. (1998). Doing grounded theory: Issues and discussions. Mill Valley, CA: Sociology Press.

Glaser. B.G., Ph.D. (2001) The Grounded Theory Perspective: Conceptualization contrasted with description. Mill Valley, CA: Sociology Press

Hansen, John Mark (1991). Gaining Access: Congress and the Farm Lobby, (1919-1981). Chicago: University of Chicago Press.

Heider, Fritz (1944) "Social Perception and Phenomenal Causality," Psychological Review , Vol. 51 (November 1944), (pp. 358-374).

Heider, Fritz (1958), The Psychology of Interpersonal Relations. Lawrence Erlbaum Associates, Inc.: Hillsdale, New Jersey.

Heilbrunn, Jacob (1994). Can Leadership be Studied? The Wilson Quarterly v. 18 (Spring 1994, pp. 65-72).

Hersey, P. & Blanchard, K. (1988). Management of organizational behavior utilizing human resources. Englewood Cliffs: Prentice Hall.

Holland, S. (1999, Spring). So Many Voices in My Head. Cross Currents, (pp. 49-72). Retrieved July 7, 2004, from Questia database, http://www.questia.com.

Ireh, Maduakolam & Bailey, Joseph (1999). A Study of Super-intendent's Change Leadership Styles Using the Situational Leadership Model. American Secondary Education (Sum 1999) v27 n4. (pp. 22-32).

Krantz, James. (1990). "3 Lessons from the Field: An Essay on the Crisis of Leadership in Contemporary Organizations." Journal of Applied Behavioral Science. Vol. 26, No. 1. (pp. 49-64).

Lasswell, Harold D., & Kaplan, Abraham (1950). Power and Society. New Haven, CT: Yale University Press.

Latham, Earl (1956). "The Group Basis of Politics" in Political Behavior, ed. Heinz Eulau, Samuel J. Eldersveld, & Morris Janowitz. New York: Free Press, (pp. 239)

March, James G., & Simon, Herbert A. (1957). Organizations. New York, John Wiley & Sons, Inc.

Matta, Seppo, & Ojala Timo (1999). A challenge for the balanced success in the public sector-towards more proactive strategic management. Research Reports 14/99. Ministry of Finance: Helsinki.

Merton, R. K. (1957), Social Theory and Social Structure. Chicago: Free Press.

McClelland, David. C. (1975). Power: The inner experience. New York: Irvington.

Parsons, Talcott (1968). The Structure of Social Action. New York: Free Press, (1968); 1st pub. (1937)

Patnode, Gerald R. (1998). Evaluation of the Effectiveness of Social Intervention

Programs in Targeted Sections of Baltimore County. Baltimore, MD: Baltimore County Government Office of Housing and Community Development.

Rosenbach, William E., & Robert L. Taylor, (1998). (Eds), Contemporary Issues in Leadership. 4th ed. Boulder, CO: Westview Press.

Schein, E. H. (1973). Management development as a process of influence. In Changing

Organizational Behavior, ed. By A. C. Barlett & T. A. Kayser, Prentice Hall, New York.

Sentis, K. P. & Burnstein, E. (1979). Remembering schema-consistent information: Effects of a balance schema on recognition memory. Journal of Personality and Social Psychology, 37, 2200-2211.

Simmons, O., Ph.D., (1995). Using grounded theory in the managing diversity context. In Glaser, B. G., Ph.D. (Ed.), Grounded theory 1984-1994. Mill Valley, CA: Sociology Press.

Simmons, Odis E., & Gregory, Toni A. (2003, September). Grounded action: Achieving optimal and sustainable change. (51 paragraphs). Forum Qualitative

Sozialforschung/Forum: Qualitative Social Research (On-Line Journal), 4(3) Available at: http://www.qualitative-research.net/fqs-texte/3-03/03simmonsgregory-e.htm. (Date of access: March 20, 2004).

Simon, H.A. (1957). Models of Man. New York: Wiley. (pp. 287).

Smith, Mark (2000). American Business and Political Power. Chicago: University of Chicago Press.

Stogdill, Ralph M. (1959). Individual Behavior and Group Achievement: A Theory, The Experimental Evidence. Author. Oxford University Press. Place of Publication: New York.

Stone, Deborah (2002). Policy Paradox, The Art of Political Decision-Making. Revised edition. New York: W.W. Norton & Company.

Stringer, E. T. (1996). Action research: A handbook for practitioners. Thousand Oaks, CA: Sage Publications, Inc.

Tuckman B. W. (1965). "Developmental sequence in small groups". Psychological Bulletin, (pp. 63, 384-99).

Vroom, V.H. & Jago, A.G. (1995). "Situation Effects and Levels of Analysis is in the Study of Leader Participation", Leadership Quarterly, 6(2), (pp. 169-81).

Wang, J. P. (2006) Crusading: A Grounded Theory of Persistent Participation in Organizational Activities., Fielding Graduate University. Doctoral Dissertation.

Walzer, N. (Ed.), (1996). Community Strategic Visioning Programs. Westport, CT: Praeger Publishers.

Waste, Robert J. (1987). Power and Pluralism in American Cities: Researching the Urban Laboratory. Greenwood Press: New York

Wilson, Graham K. (1990). Interest Groups. Cambridge, MA: Basil Blackwell.

Wright, John R. (1996). Interest Groups and Congress. Needham Heights, MA: Allyn Bacon.

Yukl, G. (June 1989). "Managerial Leadership: A Review of Theory and Research Journal of Management", (p. 274).

www.ingramcontent.com/pod-product-compliance
Lightning Source LLC
Chambersburg PA
CBHW030431290526
45786CB00001B/228